Focus on Grammar

A **HIGH-INTERMEDIATE** Course for Reference and Practice

VOLUME B

FOCUS ON GRAMMAR

A **HIGH-INTERMEDIATE** Course for Reference and Practice

SECOND EDITION

Marjorie Fuchs

Margaret Bonner

To the memory of my parents, Edith and Joseph Fuchs—MF

To my parents, Marie and Joseph Maus, and to my son, Luke Frances—MB

FOCUS ON GRAMMAR: A HIGH-INTERMEDIATE COURSE
FOR REFERENCE AND PRACTICE, VOLUME B

Pearson Education, 10 Bank Street, White Plains, NY 10606

Editorial director: Allen Ascher
Executive editor: Louisa Hellegers
Director of design and production: Rhea Banker
Development editor: Françoise Leffler
Production manager: Alana Zdinak
Managing editor: Linda Moser
Senior production editors: Sandra Pike and Virginia Bernard
Senior manufacturing manager: Patrice Fraccio
Manufacturing manager: David Dickey
Photo research: Karen Pugliano
Cover design: Rhea Banker
Cover image: *Elm, Middleton Woods, Yorkshire,*
    7 November 1980. Copyright © Andy Goldsworthy
    from his book *A Collaboration with Nature,*
    Harry N. Abrams, 1990.
Text design: Charles Yuen
Text composition: Preface, Inc.
Illustrators: Ronald Chironna: pp. 337, 357, 358; Brian Hughes:
    p. 236; Andy Myer: p. 342; Ortelius Design, Inc.: p. 321; Dusan
    Petricic; pp. 240, 246, 314, 315, 335, 346, 368, 399, 411, 412.
Photo credits: See p. xiv.

ISBN 0-201-38303-9

1 2 3 4 5 6 7 8 9 10—CRK—04 03 02 01 00 99

CONTENTS

PART IX

CONDITIONALS

PART X

INDIRECT SPEECH AND EMBEDDED QUESTIONS

APPENDICES

ABOUT THE AUTHORS

Marjorie Fuchs has taught ESL at New York City Technical College and LaGuardia Community College of the City University of New York and EFL at the Sprach Studio Lingua Nova in Munich, Germany. She holds a Master's Degree in Applied English Linguistics and a Certificate in TESOL from the University of Wisconsin–Madison. She has authored or co-authored many widely used ESL textbooks, notably *On Your Way: Building Basic Skills in English, Crossroads, Top Twenty ESL Word Games: Beginning Vocabulary Development, Around the World: Pictures for Practice, Families: Ten Card Games for Language Learners, Focus on Grammar: An Intermediate Course for Reference and Practice*, and the workbooks to the *Longman Dictionary of American English*, the *Longman Photo Dictionary, The Oxford Picture Dictionary*, and the *Vistas* series.

Margaret Bonner has taught ESL at Hunter College and the Borough of Manhattan Community College of the City University of New York, at Taiwan National University in Taipei, and at Virginia Commonwealth University in Richmond. She holds a Master's Degree in Library Science from Columbia University, and she has done work towards a Ph.D. in English Literature at the Graduate Center of the City University of New York. She has contributed to a number of ESL and EFL projects, including *Making Connections, On Your Way*, and the Curriculum Renewal Project in Oman, where she wrote textbooks, workbooks, and teachers manuals for the national school system. She authored *Step into Writing: A Basic Writing Text*, and co-authored *Focus on Grammar: An Intermediate Course for Reference and Practice* and *The Oxford Picture Dictionary Intermediate Workbook*.

INTRODUCTION

THE **FOCUS ON GRAMMAR** SERIES

Focus on Grammar: A High-Intermediate Course for Reference and Practice, Second Edition, is part of the four-level **Focus on Grammar** series. Written by practicing ESL professionals, the series focuses on English grammar through lively listening, speaking, reading, and writing activities. Each of the four Student Books is accompanied by an Answer Key, a Workbook, an Audio Program (cassettes or CDs), a Teacher's Manual, and a CD–ROM. Each Student Book can stand alone as a complete text in itself, or it can be used as part of the series.

BOTH CONTROLLED AND COMMUNICATIVE PRACTICE

Research in applied linguistics suggests that students expect and need to learn the formal rules of a language. However, students need to practice new structures in a variety of contexts to help them internalize and master them. To this end, **Focus on Grammar** provides an abundance of both controlled and communicative exercises so that students can bridge the gap between knowing grammatical structures and using them. The many communicative activities in each unit enable students to personalize what they have learned in order to talk to each other with ease about hundreds of everyday issues.

A UNIQUE FOUR-STEP APPROACH

The series follows a unique four-step approach. In the first step, **grammar in context,** new structures are shown in the natural context of passages, articles, and dialogues. This is followed by a **grammar presentation** of structures in clear and accessible grammar charts, notes, and examples. The third step is **focused practice** of both form and meaning in numerous and varied controlled exercises. In the fourth step, **communication practice,** students use the new structures freely and creatively in motivating, open-ended activities.

A COMPLETE CLASSROOM TEXT AND REFERENCE GUIDE

A major goal in the development of **Focus on Grammar** has been to provide Student Books that serve not only as vehicles for classroom instruction but also as resources for reference and self-study. In each Student Book, the combination of grammar charts, grammar notes, and expansive appendices provides a complete and invaluable reference guide for the student.

THOROUGH RECYCLING

Underpinning the scope and sequence of the series as a whole is the belief that students need to use target structures many times in many contexts at increasing levels of difficulty. For this reason new grammar is constantly recycled so that students will feel thoroughly comfortable with it.

COMPREHENSIVE TESTING PROGRAM

SelfTests at the end of each part of the Student Book allow for continual assessment of progress. In addition, diagnostic and final tests in the Teacher's Manual provide a ready-made, ongoing evaluation component for each student.

THE **HIGH-INTERMEDIATE** STUDENT BOOK

Focus on Grammar: A High-Intermediate Course for Reference and Practice, Second Edition, is divided into ten parts comprising twenty-nine units. Each part contains grammatically related units with each unit focusing on a specific grammatical structure. Where appropriate, contrast units present contrasting forms (for example, the present perfect and the simple past tense). Each unit has a major theme relating the exercises to one another. All units have the same clear, easy-to-follow format:

GRAMMAR IN CONTEXT

Grammar in Context presents the grammar focus of the unit in a natural context. The texts, all of which are recorded, present language in various formats. These include newspaper and magazine excerpts, Web sites, newsletters, advertisements, brochures, and other formats that students encounter in their day-to-day lives. In addition to presenting grammar in context, this introductory section raises student motivation and provides an opportunity for incidental learning and lively classroom discussions. Topics are varied, ranging from people's names, friendship, and saving money to skydiving, body art, and feng shui. Each text is preceded by a pre-reading activity called **Before You Read**. Pre-reading questions create interest, elicit students' knowledge about the topic, help point out features of the text, and lead students to make predictions about the reading.

GRAMMAR PRESENTATION

This section is made up of grammar charts, notes, and examples. The Grammar **charts** focus on the form of the unit's target structure. The clear and easy-to-understand boxes present each grammatical form in all its combinations. Affirmative and negative statements, *yes/no* and *wh-* questions, short answers, and contractions are presented for all tenses and modals covered. These charts provide students with a clear visual reference for each new structure.

The Grammar **notes** and **examples** that follow the charts focus on the meaning and use of the structure. Each note gives a clear explanation of the grammar point, and is always accompanied by one or more examples. Where appropriate, timelines help illustrate the meaning of verb tenses and their relationship to one another. *Be careful!* notes alert students to common ESL/EFL errors. Usage Notes provide guidelines for using and understanding different levels of formality and correctness. Pronunciation Notes are provided when appropriate. Reference Notes provide cross-references to related units and the Appendices.

FOCUSED PRACTICE

The exercises in this section provide practice for all uses of the structure presented in the Grammar Presentation. Each Focused Practice section begins with a "for recognition only" exercise called **Discover the Grammar**. Here, students are expected to recognize either the form of the structure or its meaning without having to produce any language. This activity raises awareness of the structures as it builds confidence.

Following the Discover the Grammar activity are exercises that practice the grammar in a controlled, but still contextualized, environment. The exercises proceed from simpler to more complex. There is a large variety of exercise types including fill-in-the-blanks, matching, multiple choice, question and sentence formation, and editing (error analysis). Exercises are cross-referenced to the appropriate grammar notes so that students can review the notes if necessary. As with the Grammar in Context, students are exposed to many different written formats, including letters, electronic bulletin boards, journal entries, resumes, charts, graphs, schedules, and news articles. Many exercises are art-based, providing a rich and interesting context for meaningful practice. All Focused Practice exercises are suitable for self-study or homework. A complete **Answer Key** is provided in a separate booklet.

COMMUNICATION PRACTICE

The exercises in this section are intended for in-class use. The first exercise is **Listening**. After having had exposure to and practice with the grammar in its written form, students now have the opportunity to check their aural comprehension. Students hear a variety of listening formats, including conversations, television scripts, weather forecasts, interviews, and flight announcements. After listening to the recording (or hearing the teacher read the tapescript, which can be found in the Teacher's Manual), students complete a task that focuses on either the form or the meaning of the structure. It is suggested that students be allowed to hear the text as many times as they wish to complete the task successfully.

The listening exercise is followed by a variety of activities that provide students with the opportunity to use the grammar in open-ended, interactive ways. Students work in pairs or small groups in interviews, surveys, opinion polls, information gaps, discussions, role plays, games, and problem-solving activities. The activities are fun and engaging and offer ample opportunity for self-expression and cross-cultural comparison. The final exercise in this section is always **Writing**, in which students practice using the structure in a variety of written formats.

REVIEW OR SELFTEST

After the last unit of each part, there is a review feature that can be used as a self-test. The exercises in this section test the form and use of the grammar content of the part. These tests include questions in the format of the Structure and Written Expression sections of the TOEFL®. An **Answer Key** is provided after each test, with cross-references to units for easy review.

FROM GRAMMAR TO WRITING

At the end of each part, there is a writing section called From Grammar to Writing in which students are guided to use the grammar structures in a piece of extended writing. Formats include a personal letter, a business letter, a summary, a report, and an essay. Students practice pre-writing strategies such as brainstorming, free writing, constructing a time line, using a Venn diagram, and outlining. Each writing section concludes with peer review and editing.

APPENDICES

The Appendices provide useful information, such as lists of common irregular verbs, common adjective-plus-preposition combinations, and spelling and pronunciation rules. The Appendices can help students do the unit exercises, act as a springboard for further classroom work, and serve as a reference source.

NEW IN THIS EDITION

In response to users' requests, this edition has:

- new and updated texts for Grammar in Context
- pre-reading questions
- a new easy-to-read format for grammar notes and examples
- cross-references that link exercises to corresponding grammar notes
- more photos and art
- more recorded exercises
- more information gap exercises
- more editing (error analysis) exercises
- a writing exercise in each unit
- a From Grammar to Writing section at the end of each part

SUPPLEMENTARY COMPONENTS

All supplementary components of *Focus on Grammar, Second Edition,* —the Audio Program (cassettes or CDs), the Workbook, and the Teacher's Manual—are tightly keyed to the Student Book. Along with the CD-ROM, these components provide a wealth of practice and an opportunity to tailor the series to the needs of each individual classroom.

AUDIO PROGRAM

All of the Listening exercises as well as the Grammar in Context passages and other appropriate exercises are recorded on cassettes and CDs. The symbol ▭ appears next to these activities. The scripts appear in the Teacher's Manual and may be used as an alternative way of presenting these activities.

WORKBOOK

The Workbook accompanying *Focus on Grammar: A High-Intermediate Course for Reference and Practice, Second Edition,* provides a wealth of additional exercises appropriate for self-study of the target grammar of each unit in the Student Book. Most of the exercises are fully contextualized. Themes of the Workbook exercises are typically a continuation or a spin-off of the corresponding Student Book unit themes. There are also ten tests, one for each of the ten Student Book parts. These tests have questions in the format of the Structure and Written Expression section of the TOEFL®. Besides reviewing the material in the Student Book, these questions provide invaluable practice to those who are interested in taking this widely administered test.

TEACHER'S MANUAL

The Teacher's Manual, divided into five parts, contains a variety of suggestions and information to enrich the material in the Student Book. The first part gives general suggestions for each section of a typical unit. The next part offers practical teaching suggestions and cultural information to accompany specific material in each unit. The Teacher's Manual also provides ready-to-use diagnostic and final tests for each of the ten parts of the Student Book. In addition, a complete script of the Listening exercises is provided, as is an answer key for the diagnostic and final tests.

CD-ROM

The *Focus on Grammar* CD-ROM provides individualized practice with immediate feedback. Fully contextualized and interactive, the activities broaden and extend practice of the grammatical structures in the reading, listening, and writing skill areas. The CD-ROM includes grammar review, review tests, and all relevant reference material from the Student Book. It can also be used alongside the *Longman Interactive American Dictionary* CD-ROM.

CREDITS

Grateful acknowledgment is given to the following for providing photographs:

p. 226 Alan D. Carey/PhotoDisc, Inc.; **p. 236** Zigy Kaluzny/Tony Stone Images; **p. 239** Gala/SuperStock, Inc.; **p. 249** Corbis/Kevin Schafer; **p. 250** Corbis/Peter Guttman; **p. 255** Art Resource, N.Y.; **p. 257** Library of Congress; **p. 278** Corbis/Tiziana and Gianni Baldizzone; **p. 285** Corbis/AFP; **p. 286** AP Photo/NASA; **p. 292** Chris Bjornberg/ Photo Researchers, Inc.; **p. 296** Suza Scalora/PhotoDisc, Inc.; **p. 297** *(top)* Bob Galbraith/AP Wide World Photos, *(center)* CMCD/PhotoDisc, Inc.; **p. 309** Courtesy Korea National Tourism Organization; **p. 318** Vince Streano/Tony Stone Images; **pp. 326–327** RubberBall Productions; **p. 349** *(top)* Springer/ Corbis-Bettman, *(bottom)* Corbis-Bettman; **p. 378** StockTrek/PhotoDisc, Inc.; **p. 379** National Oceanic and Atmospheric Administration; **p. 386** RubberBall Productions; **p. 387** *(top)* PhotoDisc, Inc., *(center)* Courtesy of PNI, *(bottom)* Tony Freeman/PhotoEdit; **pp. 390–391** Richard Cash/PhotoEdit; **p. 418** Stan Wakefield/Pearson Education/PH College.

ACKNOWLEDGMENTS

Before acknowledging the many people who have contributed to the second edition of *Focus on Grammar: A High-Intermediate Course for Reference and Practice*, we wish to express our gratitude to those who worked on the FIRST EDITION, and whose influence is still present in the new work.

Our continuing thanks to:

- **Joanne Dresner,** who initiated the project and helped conceptualize the general approach of *Focus on Grammar*.

- **Joan Saslow,** our editor, for helping to bring the first edition to fruition.

- **Sharon Hilles,** our grammar consultant, for her insight and advice.

Writing a SECOND EDITION has given us the wonderful opportunity to update the book and implement valuable feedback from teachers who have been using *Focus on Grammar*.

We wish, first of all, to acknowledge the following consultants and reviewers for reading the manuscript and offering many useful suggestions:

- CONSULTANTS: **Marcia Edwards Hijaab**, Henrico County Schools, Richmond, Virginia; **Tim Rees**, Transworld Schools, Boston; **Alison Rice**, Director of the International English Language Institute, Hunter College, New York; **Ellen Shaw**, University of Nevada, Las Vegas.

- REVIEWERS: **Daniel Chapuis**, English Language Institute, Queens College, CUNY; **Jeffrey Di Iuglio**, Harvard I.E.L.; **William Hall**, Houston Community College; **D. Smith**, English Language Institute, University of Pittsburgh; **Mark Stepner**, SCALE, the Somerville Center for Adult Learning Experiences, Somerville, Massachusetts; **Dee Strouse**, English Language Institute, University of Pittsburgh; **Paula Undeweiser**, University of California at Irvine; **Ellen Yaniv**, Boston University, CELOP.

We are also grateful to the following editors and colleagues:

- **Françoise Leffler**, editor *extraordinaire*, for her dedication, her keen ear, and her sense of style. We also appreciate her unstinting attention to detail and her humor, which had us looking forward to her calls. The book is undoubtedly better for her efforts.

- **Louisa Hellegers**, for being accessible and responsive to individual authors while coordinating the many complex aspects of this project.

(continued on next page)

- **Virginia Bernard** and **Sandra Pike**, for piloting the book through its many stages of production.

- **Irene Schoenberg**, author of the Basic level of *Focus on Grammar*, for generously sharing her experience in teaching our first edition and for her enthusiastic support.

Finally, we are grateful, as always, to **Rick Smith** and **Luke Frances**, for their helpful input and for standing by and supporting us as we navigated our way through another *FOG*.

M.F. and M.B.

THE STORY BEHIND THE COVER

The photograph on the cover is the work of **Andy Goldsworthy**, an innovative artist who works exclusively with natural materials to create unique outdoor sculpture, which he then photographs. Each Goldsworthy sculpture communicates the artist's own "sympathetic contact with nature" by intertwining forms and shapes structured by natural events with his own creative perspective. Goldsworthy's intention is not to "make his mark on the landscape, but to create a new perception and an evergrowing understanding of the land."

So, too, *Focus on Grammar* takes grammar found in its most natural context and expertly reveals its hidden structure and meaning. It is our hope that students everywhere will also develop a new perception and an evergrowing understanding of the world of grammar.

PART

VII

MODALS:
REVIEW AND EXPANSION

15 MODALS AND MODAL-LIKE VERBS: REVIEW

GRAMMAR **IN CONTEXT**

BEFORE YOU READ Where can you find a page like the one below? What kind of information do you expect it to have?

Read the TV schedule.

Must-See TV FRIDAY HIGHLIGHTS

NOWHERE TO HIDE 9 P.M. 13
It's the fastest animal in the world. It **can run** up to 70 m.p.h. It **can climb** trees and even **swim**, and still the cheetah **may become** extinct. You **don't have to travel** to Africa to find out why. Watch "The Big Cat" and learn why this beautiful animal is

CRITIC'S CHOICE 9 P.M. 4
Can't decide what to watch? You **shouldn't miss** tonight's "Medics." Dr. Wing and Dr. Miles **might** finally **get married**. Then again, they **might not**. A flu epidemic means that Wing **must not leave** the hospital. **Can** Wing and Miles **find** a way to the altar, or **do** we **have to wait** until next season?

MOVIE CLASSIC 10 P.M. 7
In "It **Has to Be** You," baseball star Rob Gold **can't hit** a ball anymore. He **has to face** the fact that his career **might be** over. Then he meets a sports psychologist. Soon, Rob **is able to hit** the ball out of the park, but he **can't strike up** a romance with the beautiful psychologist.

AGAINST THE LAW 8 P.M. 4
Who's been killing the members of a prestigious law firm? It **may be** a dissatisfied client, or it

might even **be** the head of the firm. It **couldn't be** that cute new law school graduate, or **could** it? You **won't be able to guess**. "You**'d Better Not Look**" will keep you in the dark until the very end.

CARTOON CRISIS 7 P.M. 5
Linda decides the Stimpsons **can't be** her real family. The only smart one in America's favorite cartoon family, Linda believes that her real family **must live** somewhere in Centerville, and she **has got to find** them. **Could** anyone **change** her mind? Her dad, Hector, **might**. Watch this episode of "The Stimpsons" to find out.

GRAMMAR **PRESENTATION**
MODALS AND MODAL-LIKE VERBS: REVIEW

ABILITY: *CAN AND COULD*

SUBJECT	MODAL	BASE FORM OF VERB	
She	can (not)	act.	
	could (not)	act	last year.

ABILITY: *BE ABLE TO**

SUBJECT	BE ABLE TO		BASE FORM OF VERB
She	is (not) was (not)	able to	act.

ADVICE: *SHOULD, OUGHT TO, HAD BETTER*

SUBJECT	MODAL	BASE FORM OF VERB	
You	should (not) ought to had better (not)	watch	this TV show.

NECESSITY: *MUST AND CAN'T*

SUBJECT	MODAL	BASE FORM OF VERB
You	must (not) can't	go.

NECESSITY: *HAVE (GOT) TO**

SUBJECT	HAVE (GOT) TO	BASE FORM OF VERB
We	(don't) have to	go.
He	has (got) to	

*Unlike modals, which have one form, *be* in *be able to* and *have* in *have (got) to* change for different subjects and tenses.

FUTURE POSSIBILITY: *MAY, MIGHT, COULD*

SUBJECT	MODAL	BASE FORM OF VERB	
You	may (not) might (not) could	start	at 8:00.

(continued on next page)

ASSUMPTIONS: MAY, MIGHT, COULD, MUST, CAN'T

SUBJECT	MODAL	BASE FORM OF VERB	
They	**may (not)** **might (not)** **could (not)** **must (not)** **can't**	**be**	actors.

ASSUMPTIONS: HAVE (GOT) TO

SUBJECT	HAVE (GOT) TO	BASE FORM OF VERB	
They	**have (got) to**	**be**	actors.
He	**has (got) to**		an actor.

NOTES

EXAMPLES

1. Modals are auxiliary ("helping") verbs that we use to express

  a. Social functions such as giving advice.

- You **should watch** this program.

  b. Logical possibilities such as making assumptions.

- It **could be** the best of the season.

REMEMBER: Modals have <u>only one form</u>. They do not have an *-s* in the third person singular. The verb following the modal is the base form.

- She **might tape** it.
 NOT ~~She mights tape it.~~
 NOT ~~She might to tape it.~~

2. Use *can* or *be able to* to describe <u>present ability</u>.

- She **can sing**, but she **can't dance**.
- We **aren't able to get** Channel 11.

USAGE NOTE: *Can* is used more frequently than *be able to* in the <u>present tense</u>.

Use *could* and *was / were able to* for <u>past ability</u>.

- Before she took lessons, she **could sing**, but she **wasn't able to dance** well.

Use the correct form of *be able to* for <u>all other tenses</u>.

- Since her lessons, she **has been able to get** good roles on TV.

3. Use *should* and *ought to* to give advice.

USAGE NOTE: *Should* is more formal than *ought to*.

Use *had better* for urgent advice—when you believe that something bad will happen if the person does not follow the advice.

Use *should* to ask for advice.

Use *shouldn't* and *had better not* for negative statements.

- You **should watch** "Mystery!" tonight.
- Terri **ought to watch** it, too.

- You**'d better stop** watching so much TV or your grades will suffer.

- **Should** I **buy** a new TV set?

- You **shouldn't get** it repaired.
- You**'d better not stay** up too late.

4. Use *have to*, *have got to*, and *must* to express necessity.

USAGE NOTES:
a. *Have to* is the most common expression in everyday use.

b. *Have got to* is usually used only in spoken English and informal writing. When it is used in spoken English, it often expresses strong feeling on the part of the speaker.

c. *Must* is used to express obligation in writing, including official forms, signs, and notices.

When *must* is used in spoken English, the speaker

- usually is in a position of power.

- is expressing urgent necessity.

Must and *have got to* refer only to the present or the future.

Use the correct form of *have to* for all other tenses.

- You **have to press** *Start* to begin recording.

- You**'ve got to see** this! It's really funny!

- You **must have** your VCR on Channel 3 in order to record.
  (VCR instruction manual)

- You **must go** to bed right now, Tommy!
  (mother talking to her young son)
- You really **must talk** to your boss about a raise.
  (friend talking to a friend)

- You **must go** to bed now.
- You**'ve got to get up** early tomorrow.

- He **had to go** to bed early last night.
- She **has had to miss** her favorite program since she enrolled in that class.

(continued on next page)

▶ **BE CAREFUL!** The meanings of *must not* and *don't have to* are very different.

Must not expresses <u>prohibition</u>.

- He **must not watch** that program.
  (He is not allowed to watch the program.)

Don't have to expresses that something is <u>not necessary</u>.

- He **doesn't have to watch** that program.
  (It isn't necessary for him to watch it, but he can watch it if he wants to.)

USAGE NOTE: We often use *can't* instead of *must not* to express <u>prohibition in spoken English</u>.

- He **can't stay** up past 10:00.

---

5. Use *may*, *might*, and *could* to talk about <u>future possibility</u>.

- The show **may start** at 10:00. I'm not sure.
- It **might be** very good.
- It **could win** an award.

Use *may not* and *might not* to express the possibility that something <u>will not happen</u>.

- It **may not make** people laugh.
- It **might not be** good.

▶ **BE CAREFUL!** *Couldn't* means that something is <u>impossible</u>.

- It **couldn't start** at 10:00. The news is on then.

USAGE NOTE: We usually do not begin <u>questions about possibility</u> with *may*, *might*, or *could*. Instead we use *will* or *be going to* and phrases such as *Do you think . . . ?* or *Is it possible that . . . ?*

However, we often use *may*, *might*, or *could* <u>in short answers</u> to these questions.

A: *Do you think* she'll win an award?
B: She **might**. She did a great acting job.

A: *Is* Midge *going to star* in the show?
B: She **may**. She hasn't decided yet.

6. We often make **assumptions**, or "best guesses," based on information we have. The modal that we choose depends on how certain we are about the assumption.

	100% certain	
AFFIRMATIVE	↑	**NEGATIVE**
must		**can't, couldn't**
have (got) to		**must not**
may		**may not**
might, could	↓	**might not**
	0% certain	

a. Use **must**, **have to**, and **have got to** to state affirmative conclusions when you are almost 100% certain that something is true.

- She **must live** here. Her name's on the door.
- She **has to be** home. She just answered the phone.
- She**'s got to know** something. She's his wife.

When you are less certain, use **may**, **might**, and **could** to express affirmative possibilities.

- He **may be** the murderer. He looks guilty.
- He **might know** something about the crime. He lives right next door.
- He **could be** home now. The lights are on.

b. Use **can't** and **couldn't** to express negative conclusions when you are almost 100% certain that something is impossible.

- They **can't be** guilty. They weren't even in the city when the crime occurred.
- They **couldn't own** a gun. It just isn't like them.

Use **must not** when you are slightly less certain.

- You **must not know** them very well. You've only met them twice.

When you are even less certain, use **may not** and **might not** to express negative possibilities.

- We **may not have** enough evidence. No one saw the suspect.
- That **might not be** important. We have his fingerprints.

FOCUSED PRACTICE

1 DISCOVER THE GRAMMAR

Read the article. Underline the modals and modal-like verbs. Also underline the verbs that follow.

TV LITERACY

The average U.S. teen-ager might watch as many as 18,000 hours of TV by the time he or she graduates. You may think that anyone who watches this much TV has got to understand how it works. However, most of us (not just teenagers) can't recognize many of the messages TV is sending. For this reason, many experts think that everyone should become "TV literate." People who are television literate are able to understand how TV messages influence an audience. They don't have to believe everything they see on the tube. Here are some things you ought to know about television.

• TV networks have to make money by selling time to advertisers. This fact influences all commercial TV. A drama writer, for example, may avoid topics that could embarrass the advertiser sponsoring the program.

• TV's world is not real. This might sound obvious, but you ought to remind yourself often of this fact. After all, when you see something, you feel that it must be the real thing. You've got to remember that the cereal commercial uses white glue, not milk, so the cereal doesn't get soggy the way it does in real life.

• TV uses specific techniques and you can learn to identify them. Lighting, camera angles, and music have got the ability to make things seem beautiful, frightening, or funny. They can also make you feel that you must buy a certain product.

Get literate, and you'll be able to enjoy TV, without being its victim.   ❖

—SEYMOUR TELLY

Put the underlined verbs into the correct categories.

Ability	Advice	Necessity
_____	ought to remind	must buy
can't recognize	should become	must be
can learn	ought to know	have to buy
_____		have got to understand
_____		can learn

Future Possibility	**Assumptions**
might watch	might think
may think	
might sound	

able to enjoy
able undestand

② A NIGHT OF TV — Grammar Notes 1–6

Circle the correct words to complete these conversations.

1. **A:** What do you feel like watching?

   B: It's 7:00. We (could) / shouldn't watch "The Stimpsons." It's just starting now.

2. **A:** Do you think the Stimpsons aren't Linda's real family?

   B: They can't / (must) be. She looks just like them!

3. **A:** This show is really funny, but I may / ('ve got to) leave now, or I'll be late.

   B: No problem. I (can) / should tape the rest of the show for you.

4. **A:** There's a two-hour mystery on at 8:00.

   B: If we watch that we won't (be able to) / have to watch "Medics" at 9:00.

   A: That's what VCRs are for. We (could) / 'd better not watch one show and tape

   the other.

5. **A:** I think the law clerk is the killer.

   B: It could / (couldn't) be the clerk. She was on a plane to Barbados at the time of the

   last murder. Remember?

6. **A:** Is it OK if I turn the volume up? I can / (can't) hear what they're saying.

   B: Sure. But you 'd better / ('d better not) make it too loud, or you'll wake the baby.

7. **A:** What's the matter with Dr. Wing? He's acting kind of strange.

   B: He (must) / must not be sick. Everyone around him has the flu.

8. **A:** I'm just going to see what's on Channel 13 during this commercial.

   B: Wow! Look at that cheetah run! They (have got to) / don't have to be the fastest

   animals in the world!

(continued on next page)

9. A: Do you think that Dr. Wing and Dr. Miles will get married in this episode?

  B: They might not / should not. There are only five minutes left!

10. A: Poor Rob. It must / might be awful for an athlete to suddenly lose so many games.

  B: Don't worry. I'm sure the sports psychologist might / will be able to help him.

11. A: How can / should you watch those horror movies? They give me the creeps.

  B: You 've got to / shouldn't remember that it's all special effects.

12. A: Have they done the weather forecast yet?

  B: Yes. They say it's going to clear up by early tomorrow morning.

  A: Oh, good. That means I don't have to / must not take my umbrella.

3 WHAT COULD BE WRONG? Grammar Notes 1–6

Complete Rob's conversation with a sports psychologist. Rewrite the phrases in parentheses using modals.

ROB: That's it! I'm quitting. _____I can't do_____ this anymore.
1. (I don't have the ability to do)

DR. ANN: Oh, sure, just give up. Then _you don't have to find out_ what's
2. (you are not required to find out)

really wrong.

ROB: What else _should I do_? Wait until they trade me?
3. (do you advise that I do?)

DR. ANN: OK, _we had better_ about this. When did this start?
4. (it's a good idea for us to talk)

ROB: Three months ago. One day _I could hit_ the ball, and the
5. (I had the ability to hit)

next day _I couldn't_.
6. (I didn't have the ability)

DR. ANN: Look, you don't lose a skill overnight. _It can't happen_.
7. (It's impossible for that to happen)

But _you might stop_ hitting the ball because something is
8. (it's possible for you to stop)

bothering you. And _you might not know_ what that is yet.
9. (it's almost impossible that you know)

ROB: So, I'm a good ballplayer, but _I must be crazy_.
10. (it's almost 100% certain that I'm crazy)

DR. ANN: Rob, _you must stop_ thinking that way or
11. (it's urgent that you stop)

you might never hit another home run ever again.
12. (it's possible that you won't hit)

ROB: OK. What _should I do_?
13. (is it necessary that I do)

DR. ANN: First, _you should try_ to remember what was happening just
14. (it's a good idea for you to try)

before your problem started.

4 EDITING

Read these postings to an online message board for the TV show "Medics." Find and correct eleven mistakes in the use of modals. The first mistake is already corrected.

MEDICS BULLETIN BOARD

[Follow Ups] [Post a Reply] [Message Board Index]

Last night's "Medics" was awesome! I cried when Miles and Wing couldn't ~~to get~~ *get* married in the emergency room because that really sick patient came in. Miles abled to save the patient's life, but the priest had to leave, so they couldn't had the ceremony. Oh, well. There's always next season.

I just read in *TV Now* that the actor who plays Dr. Miles might leave the show because of a contract dispute! He have to be the most talented (and best-looking!) actor around. I love him! They better renew his contract, or I'll stop watching!

I think they ought handle more social issues on the show. They could do some episodes about AIDS or teen pregnancy. It's good when a show be able to entertain and educate at the same time.

Last episode shows Dr. Miles shaking hands with a sick patient and then eating an apple without first washing his hands. Come on now! You must not be a rocket scientist to know that you can get sick that way! The writers have better check their facts!

Help! I just started watching "Medics" and I'm confused. Can anyone tells me what the relationship is between Tania and Jax? She can be his mother, she's much too young! I suppose she might be his sister, but I'm not sure that makes any sense.

COMMUNICATION PRACTICE

5 LISTENING

Listen to part of a script from a TV series. Listen again and complete the script with the modals you hear. Listen a third time to check your answers.

MIA: I _____can't_____ stop
1.

thinking of Jessie. Where is she!?

JON: Wherever she is, she

___'s got to___ be scared.
2.

MIA: She's my baby, my little girl. She

___must not___ know that
3.

it's safe to come home.

JON: She's been missing for

twenty-two hours. Maybe we

___shouldn't___ wait until
4.

tomorrow to call the police.

MIA: I've already called them. I keep thinking that there's something I

_____could_____ or _____should_____ be doing.
5.   6.

JON: I know. Is there anything *I* _____can_____ do? _____should_____
7.   8.

I call Martine?

MIA: I've been thinking about that. We ___'ve better not___ tell Martine.
9.

JON: OK. It's your decision. Have you checked with Dylan? Jess ___might___
10.

be there.

MIA: With Dylan? She _____can't_____ be with Dylan! *(telephone rings)*
11.

I ___have to___ get that. It ___might___ be Jessie.
12.   13.

JON: It _____could_____ be the police.
14.

Read the statements and decide if they are **True (T)** *or* **False (F)**.

_T_ **15.** Jon believes Jessie is scared.

_F_ **16.** Jon wants to wait before calling the police.

_T_ **17.** Mia doesn't want to tell Martine that Jessie is missing.

_F_ **18.** Mia thinks that Jessie is with Dylan.

_F_ **19.** Jon doesn't think the police are phoning.

6 SPECULATING SPECTATORS

Work with a partner. Look at the TV listings. What types of programs do you think they are?

SATURDAY 8PM–MIDNIGHT

CHANNEL	8:00	8:30	9:00	9:30	10:00	10:30	11:00	11:30
1	Around the World		The Dark Glove ('98) Roy Collins				Live at 1	Johnny!
2	Great Performances: Vivaldi, Mozart, Stravinsky				Garden		World	Nighttime
3	To Mars and Back		King of the Jungle		The Joke's on You	How to Boil Water	The Hulk vs. Bad Boy	Pet Heroes
4	Judge Jim	Detective Ramsey	The Long Goodbye ('96) Vera Garcia, Antonio Serrano				Top Ten	Volcano
5	Boston College vs. Massachusetts				The Week that Was		The Civil War	
6	Elvis Presley: A Portrait singer's life		Recipes for Life	Ask Dr. Anne	Shadows in the Sand ('99) Crystal Powers (Part 2)			
7	Rita's World	You Guessed It!	Money Week	October Sky ('99) Laura Dern, Jake Gillenhall			A Laugh a Minute	

EXAMPLE:

A: "Around the World." What type of show is that?

B: It could be a travel show.

A: Or it might be a news show with international reports.

7 CLASS DISCUSSION: INTERNATIONAL TV

Talk about TV in a country that you know. Discuss the following questions:

- How many channels can you watch?
- How late can you watch?
- What programs do you recommend? What programs don't you recommend?
- Who are the most popular TV personalities?
- Do you have to pay tax for using a TV?
- Do you have to have any special equipment such as a satellite dish?
- Can you watch programs from other countries?
- Should foreign shows have subtitles, or should they be dubbed?

8 ROLE PLAY

Work with a partner. Role-play one of these story lines from several TV series. Use modals.

- Brad, a student, might fail this semester. He hasn't been able to concentrate since he and Ellen broke up. He has just received a note that says, "I love you. I'm sorry." He thinks the note must be from Ellen. He rushes to her apartment. Meanwhile, Ellen (who did *not* send the note), leaves a message on Brad's answering machine: "You've got to return the $100 I loaned you or I'll lose my apartment."

Role-play Brad's conversation with Ellen.

- Paula's invention will earn her millions of dollars once she gets a patent. Then someone steals the disk with all the information. (Forgetful Paula didn't copy the disk.) Next door, Tory watches at his window all day and never goes out. Paula must convince him to tell her what he saw. Tory saw a woman enter Paula's house, but she looked just like the woman who terrified him as a child. He doesn't want any trouble.

Role-play Paula's conversation with Tory.

- Raul doesn't really want a job, but his mother, a nurse, has insisted that he interview for a receptionist position in the emergency room of their local hospital. He hopes he doesn't get the job but he has to go through the interview anyway. The emergency room is very busy, and the person who interviews Raul is desperate for anyone to take the job.

Role-play the interview.

9 WRITING

Choose one of the story lines from Exercise 8. Write a short script. Use modals. You can use the script in Exercise 5 as a model.

ADVISABILITY AND OBLIGATION IN THE PAST

GRAMMAR **IN CONTEXT**

BEFORE YOU READ   What are some examples of typical regrets that people have? Why do you think the article is called "Useless Regrets"?

Read this article from a popular psychology magazine.

USELESS *Regrets*

For all sad words of tongue or pen
The saddest are these:
"It **might have been."**
　　　　　　　—John Greenleaf Whittier

Not only the saddest, but perhaps the most destructive. According to recent ideas in psychology, our feelings are mainly the result of the way we *think* about reality, not reality itself.

According to Nathan S. Kline, M.D., it's not unusual to feel deep regret about things in the past that you think you **should have done** and did not do—or the opposite, about things you did do and feel you **should not have done**. In fact, we learn by thinking about past mistakes. For example, a student who fails a test learns that he or she **should have studied** more and can improve on the next test.

However, thinking too much about past mistakes and missed opportunities can create such bad feelings that people become paralyzed and can't move on with their lives. Arthur Freeman, Ph.D., and Rose DeWolf have labeled this process "woulda/coulda/shoulda thinking," and they have written an entire book about this type of disorder.

I could have become a doctor.

My parents **might have encouraged** *me more.*

I **ought to have applied** *to college.*

I shouldn't have missed that opportunity.

I could have been rich and famous by now.

(continued on next page)

USELESS Regrets

(continued)

In *Woulda/Coulda/Shoulda: Overcoming Regrets, Mistakes, and Missed Opportunities*, Freeman and DeWolf suggest challenging regrets with specifics. "Instead of saying, 'I **should have done better**,'" they suggest, "Write down an example of a way in which you **might have done** better. Exactly what **should** you **have done** to produce the desired result? Did you have the skills, money, experience, etc. at the time?" In the case of the student who **should have studied** more, perhaps on that occasion it was not really possible.

When people examine their feelings of regret about the past, they often find that many of them are simply not based in fact. A mother regrets missing a football game in which her son's leg was injured. She blames herself and the officials. "I **should have gone**," she keeps telling herself. "I **could have prevented** the injury. They **might** at least **have telephoned** me as soon as it happened." Did she *really* have the power to prevent her son's injury? **Should** the officials **have called** her *before* looking at the injury? Probably not.

Once people realize how unrealistic their feelings of regret are, they are more ready to let go of them. Cognitive psychologist David Burns, M.D., suggests specific strategies for dealing with useless feelings of regret and getting on with the present. One amusing technique is to spend ten minutes a day writing down all the things you regret. Then say them all aloud (better yet, record them), and listen to yourself.

Once you listen to your own "woulda/coulda/shoulda" thoughts, it's easier to see their illogic. For example, it's unlikely that your entire career is in ruins because of one joke. You're an adult and you can choose to go out instead of cleaning house. That doesn't make you a lazy person. And your boyfriend isn't a jerk for making a single mistake.

After you recognize how foolish most feelings of regret sound, the next step is to let go of them and to start dealing with life in the present. For some, this might be harder than sighing over past errors. An Italian proverb notes, "When the ship has sunk, everyone knows how they **could have saved** it." The message from cognitive psychology is similar. It's easy to second guess about the past; the real challenge is to solve the problems you face right now.

- *I* **shouldn't have told** *that joke in the office. My career is ruined.*

- *I* **ought to have cleaned** *the house instead of going out this weekend. My mother's right. I'm just lazy.*

- *My boyfriend* **could have told** *me he was going out of town this weekend. He's an inconsiderate jerk. I* **should** *never* **have started** *going out with him.*

GRAMMAR **PRESENTATION**
ADVISABILITY AND OBLIGATION IN THE PAST:
SHOULD HAVE, OUGHT TO HAVE, COULD HAVE, MIGHT HAVE

STATEMENTS				
SUBJECT	**MODAL***	*HAVE*	**PAST PARTICIPLE**	
He	**should (not) ought (not) to could might**	**have**	**told**	her.

* *Should, ought to, could,* and *might* are modals. Modals have only one form.
They do not have *-s* in the third-person singular.

YES / NO QUESTIONS				
SHOULD	**SUBJECT**	*HAVE*	**PAST PARTICIPLE**	
Should	he	**have**	**told**	her?

SHORT ANSWERS			
AFFIRMATIVE			
Yes,	he	**should**	**have.**

SHORT ANSWERS			
NEGATIVE			
No,	he	**shouldn't**	**have.**

WH- QUESTIONS					
WH- WORD	*SHOULD*	**SUBJECT**	*HAVE*	**PAST PARTICIPLE**	
When	**should**	he	**have**	**told**	her?

CONTRACTIONS		
should have	=	**should've**
could have	=	**could've**
might have	=	**might've**
should not have	=	**shouldn't have**

NOTES	EXAMPLES
1. Use the modals *should have, ought to have, could have,* and *might have* to talk about actions and states that were <u>advisable in the past</u>. These modals often communicate a sense of regret or blame.	• I **should've applied** to college. *(I didn't apply to college, and I'm sorry.)* • I **ought to have taken** that job. *(I didn't take the job. That was a mistake.)* • She **could've gone** to a better school. *(She didn't go to a good school. Now she regrets her choice.)* • You **might've told** me. *(You didn't tell me. That was wrong.)*
2. USAGE NOTE: *Should not have* and *ought not to have* are the only forms used in <u>negative statements</u>. *Should not have* is more common. *Should (not) have* is the most common form used in <u>questions</u>.	• He **shouldn't have missed** the exam. • He **ought not to have missed** the exam. • **Should** he **have called** the teacher?
3. PRONUNCIATION NOTES: **a.** In informal speech, *have* in <u>modal phrases</u> is often pronounced like the word *of.* ▶ BE CAREFUL! Do not write *of* instead of *have* with past modals. **b.** In informal speech *to* in *ought to* is pronounced like the word *a.* ▶ BE CAREFUL! Do not write *a* instead of *to* with *ought.*	• **could have** /kʊdəv/ • I **should** *have* gone. NOT ~~I should of gone.~~ • **ought to** /ɔt̬ə/ • I **ought** *to* have gone. NOT ~~I ought a have gone.~~

REFERENCE NOTE
Could have and *might have* are also used to express speculations about the past. (*See Unit 17.*)

FOCUSED PRACTICE

1 DISCOVER THE GRAMMAR

*Read each numbered statement. Then choose the sentence (**a** or **b**) that best describes the situation.*

1. I shouldn't have called him.
   a. I called him. *(circled)*
   b. I didn't call him.

2. My parents ought to have moved away from that neighborhood.
   a. They're going to move, but they're not sure when.
   b. Moving was a good idea, but they didn't do it. *(circled)*

3. I should have told them what I thought.
   a. I didn't tell them, and now I regret it. *(circled)*
   b. I told them, and that was a big mistake.

4. We could have told you that movie was no good.
   a. We didn't know you were planning to go, so we didn't tell you. *(circled)*
   b. We haven't seen the movie yet, so we can't tell you about it.

5. He might have warned us about the traffic.
   a. He didn't know, so he couldn't tell us.
   b. He knew, but he didn't tell us. *(circled)*

6. Felicia could have been a vice president by now.
   a. Felicia didn't become a vice president. *(circled)*
   b. Felicia is a vice president.

7. I ought to have practiced more.
   a. I practiced enough.
   b. I didn't practice enough. *(circled)*

8. They shouldn't have lent him their car.
   a. They refused to lend him their car.
   b. They lent him their car. *(circled)*

2 ETHICS DISCUSSION

Grammar Notes 1–3

A class is discussing an ethical question. Complete the discussion with the correct form of the verbs in parentheses or short answers. Choose between affirmative and negative.

Problem: Greg, a college student, worked successfully for a clothing store for a year. He spent most of his salary on books and tuition. One week he wanted some extra money to buy a sweater to wear to a party. He asked for a raise, but his boss refused. The same week, Greg discovered an extra sweater in a shipment he was unpacking. It was very stylish and just his size. Greg "borrowed" it for the weekend and then brought it back. His boss found out and fired him.

(continued on next page)

TEACHER: _____Should_____ Greg's boss _____have given_____ him a raise?
1. (Should / give)

STUDENT A: Yes, he ____should have____. After all, Greg had worked there for a whole
2.

year. His boss __should'n have refused__ at that point.
3. (should / refuse)

STUDENT B: But maybe his boss couldn't afford a raise. Anyway, Greg still

____shouldn't have taken____ the sweater. It wasn't his.
4. (should / take)

TEACHER: What ____should____ he ____have done____ instead?
5. (should / do)

STUDENT C: He ____might have asked____ his boss to sell him the sweater. Then he
6. (might / ask)

____could have paid____ for it slowly, out of his salary.
7. (could / pay)

STUDENT A: He ____ought have wore____ his old clothes to the party. A new sweater just
8. (ought to / wear)

wasn't worth all this trouble.

TEACHER: Well, ____should____ Greg's boss ____have fired____ him?
9. (should / fire)

STUDENT B: No, he __shouldn't have__. Greg had been a good employee for a year.
10.

And he did bring the sweater back.

TEACHER: How ____should____ he ____have handle____ the situation?
11. (should / handle)

STUDENT C: He __ought to have warned__ him. He ____shouldn't____ just
12. (ought to / warn)

____have fired____ him without any warning.
13. (should / fire)

<hr>

❸ GRETA REGRETS

Grammar Notes 1–3

*Read the things Greta is complaining about. Rewrite all the things she regrets
about the past, using the modals in parentheses. Choose between affirmative and
negative.*

1. I didn't go to college. Now I'm unhappy with my job.

(should) __I should have gone to college.__

2. My brother quit a good job, and now he's sorry. I knew it was a mistake, but I didn't
warn him. How inconsiderate of me.

(might) __I might have warned my brother about
quiting his job.__

3. I feel sick. I ate all the chocolate.

(should) __I shouldn't have aten all the
chocolate.__

4. Christina didn't come over. She didn't even call.

(might) _Christina might have told me that she wasn't able to come over._

5. I didn't have enough money to buy the shirt. Why didn't Ed offer to lend me some?

(could) _Ed could have oled the money to buy me a shirt._

6. I jogged five miles yesterday, and now I'm exhausted.

(should) _I shouldn't have jogged five miles, because now I'm exhausted._

7. The supermarket charged me for the plastic bag. They used to be free.

(should) _I shouldn't have bought in that supermarket, they charged me for a plastic bag._

8. I didn't do the laundry yesterday, so I don't have any clean socks. Everyone else gets their laundry done on time. Why can't I?

(ought to) _I ought to have done my laundry._

9. I didn't invite Cynthia to the party. Now she's angry at me.

(should) _I should have invited Cynthia to the party._

10. Yesterday was my birthday, and my brother didn't send me a card. I'm hurt.

(might) _My brother might have send me a card on my birthday._

4 EDITING

Read this journal entry. Find and correct six mistakes in the use of modals. The first mistake is already corrected.

December 15

About a week ago, Jennifer was late for work again, and Doug, our boss, told me he

wanted to get rid of her. I was really upset. Of course, Jennifer shouldn't ~~had~~ have *been late*

so often, but he might ~~has~~ have *talked to her about the problem before he decided to let her*

go. Then he told me to make her job difficult for her so that she would quit. I just

pretended I didn't hear him. What a mistake! I ought ~~ø~~ to *have confronted him right*

away. Or I could at least have warned Jennifer. Anyway, Jennifer is still here, but now

I'm worried about my own job. Should I ~~of~~ have *told his boss? I wonder. Maybe I should*

have *handle things differently last week. The company should never ~~has~~* have *hired this guy.*

weren't

COMMUNICATION PRACTICE

5 LISTENING

Jennifer is taking some of Dr. David Burns's advice by recording all the things she regrets at the end of the day. Listen to her recording. Then listen again and check the things she did.

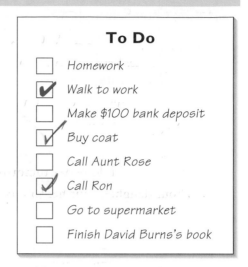

To Do

- [ ] Homework
- [x] Walk to work
- [ ] Make $100 bank deposit
- [x] Buy coat
- [ ] Call Aunt Rose
- [x] Call Ron
- [ ] Go to supermarket
- [ ] Finish David Burns's book

6 WHAT A MESS!

Work with a partner. Look at the picture of Jennifer's apartment. What should she have done? What shouldn't she have done? Write as many sentences as you can in five minutes. When you are done, compare your answers with those of your classmates.

EXAMPLE:
She should have paid the electric bill.

7 S.O.S.

How strong is your sense of obligation? Take this test and find out.

Sense of Obligation Survey (S.O.S.)

Instructions: Read each situation. Circle the letter of your most likely response.

1. You want to lose ten pounds, but you just ate a large dish of ice cream.
   a. I shouldn't have eaten the ice cream. I have no willpower.
   b. I deserve to enjoy things once in a while. I'll do better tomorrow.

2. Your daughter quit her job. Now she's unemployed.
   a. Maybe she was really unhappy at work. It's better that she left.
   b. She shouldn't have quit until she found another job.

3. You had an appointment with your doctor. You arrived on time but had to wait more than an hour.
   a. My doctor should have scheduled better. My time is valuable, too.
   b. Maybe there was an emergency. I'm sure it's not my doctor's fault.

4. You bought a coat for $140. A day later you saw it at another store for just $100.
   a. That was really bad luck.
   b. I should have looked around before I bought the coat.

5. Your brother didn't send you a birthday card.
   a. He could have at least called. He only cares about himself.
   b. Maybe he forgot. He's really been busy lately.

6. You just got back an English test. Your grade was 60 percent.
   a. That was a really difficult test.
   b. I should have studied harder.

7. You just found out that an electrician overcharged you.
   a. I should have known that was too much money.
   b. How could I have known? I'm not an expert.

8. You forgot to do some household chores that you had promised to do. Now the person you live with is angry.
   a. I shouldn't have forgotten. I'm irresponsible.
   b. I'm only human. I make mistakes.

9. You got a ticket for driving five miles per hour above the speed limit.
   a. I ought to have obeyed the speed limit.
   b. The police officer could've overlooked it and not given me the ticket. It was only five miles over the speed limit.

10. You went to the movies but couldn't get a ticket because it was sold out.
    a. I should've gone earlier.
    b. Wow! This movie is really popular!

SCORING
Give yourself one point for each of these answers:

1. a	6. b
2. b	7. a
3. a	8. a
4. b	9. a
5. a	10. a

The higher your score, the stronger your sense of obligation.

Compare your survey results with those of a classmate.

EXAMPLE:
A: What did you answer for Question 1?
B: I said I shouldn't have eaten the ice cream. What about you?

8 DILEMMAS

Work with a group. Read and discuss each case. Did the people act properly or should they have done things differently?

CASE 1

Sheila was in her last year of college when she decided to run for student council president. During her campaign, a school newspaper reporter asked her about something from her past. In high school, Sheila had once been caught cheating on a test. She had admitted her mistake and repeated the course. She never cheated again. Sheila felt that the incident was over, and she refused to answer the reporter's questions. The reporter wrote the story without telling Sheila's side, and Sheila lost the election. Her reputation at school was also damaged, and she's afraid she won't find a job easily when she graduates.

> **EXAMPLE:**
> **A:** Should Sheila have refused to answer questions about her past?
> **B:** I don't think so. She should've told her side of the story.

CASE 2

Mustafa is a social worker who cares very deeply about his clients. A few months ago, there was a fire in his office building. After the fire, the fire department declared that the building was no longer safe, and Mustafa's supervisor forbade anyone to go back for any reason. Mustafa became worried because all his clients' records were in the building. The records included names, addresses, telephone numbers, and other information Mustafa needed to help his clients. He decided it was worth the risk, and he entered the building to get them. His supervisor found out and fired Mustafa. Now he is unemployed, and his clients have a new social worker who is not as familiar with their problems as Mustafa was.

CASE 3

Pierre's wife had been sick for a long time. One day, the doctor told Pierre that there was a new medication that might save his wife. However, he warned Pierre that the medicine was very expensive. Since it was still experimental, Pierre's insurance would not pay for it. The doctor wrote a prescription, and Pierre immediately went to the pharmacy to buy the medication. He discovered that it was so expensive that he just didn't have enough money to buy it. The pharmacist would not agree to give Pierre the medication and let him pay later. Pierre decided to look for extra work on nights and weekends to pay for the medicine. However, the extra work prevented him from taking care of his wife as carefully as he had before.

9 WRITING

Use Exercise 4 as a model and write about a dilemma that you have faced. Discuss what you and others should have, might have, or could have done in the situation. When you finish writing, exchange paragraphs with another student and discuss your ideas.

SPECULATIONS AND CONCLUSIONS ABOUT THE PAST

GRAMMAR **IN CONTEXT**

BEFORE YOU READ   What do you think the design in the photograph represents? Who do you think made it? When?

*The great achievements of ancient cultures fascinate modern people.
Read one writer's theories regarding these achievements.*

Close Encounters

In 1927, Toribio Mexta Xesspe of Peru **must have been** very surprised to see lines in the shapes of huge animals and geometric forms on the ground below his airplane. Created by the ancient Nazca culture, these beautiful forms (over 13,000 of them) are too big to recognize from the ground. However, from about 600 feet in the air, the giant forms take shape. Xesspe **may have been** the first human in almost a thousand years to recognize the designs.

Since their rediscovery, many people have speculated about the Nazca lines. Without airplanes, how **could** an ancient culture **have made** these amazing pictures? What purpose **could** they **have had**?

One writer, Erich von Däniken, has a theory as amazing as the Nazca lines

themselves. According to von Däniken, visitors from other planets brought their civilization to the Earth thousands of years ago. When these astronauts visited ancient cultures here on Earth, the people of those cultures **must have believed** that they were gods. Since the Nazcans **could have built** the lines according to instructions from an aircraft,

Nazca lines

(continued on next page)

Close Encounters

(continued)

von Däniken concludes that the drawings **might have marked** a landing strip for the spacecraft of the ancient astronauts. Von Däniken writes, "The builders of the geometrical figures **may have had** no idea what they were doing. But perhaps they knew perfectly well what the 'gods' needed in order to land."

In his book *Chariots of the Gods?* (New York: Bantam, 1972) von Däniken offers many other "proofs" that ancient cultures had contact with visitors from other planets. Giant statues on Easter Island provide von Däniken with strong evidence of the astronauts' presence. Von Däniken estimates that the island **could** only **have supported** a very small population. After examining the simple tools that the islanders probably used, he concludes that even 2,000 men working day and night **could not have been** enough to carve the figures out of hard stone. In addition, he says that at least part of the population **must have worked** in the fields, **gone** fishing and **woven** cloth. Therefore, he concludes, "Two thousand men alone **could not have made** the gigantic statues."

In a later book, *In Search of Ancient Gods* (New York: Putnam, 1984), von Däniken sees additional "evidence" in a famous map created by a Turkish admiral, Piri Reis, in 1513. The map appears to include Antarctica, which was not discovered until 300 years later. Von Däniken believes that in 1513 map makers **couldn't** possibly **have had** the information shown in this map. He insists, "Whoever made it **must have been able to fly** and to take photographs." According to von Däniken, only one conclusion is possible: "To me it is obvious that extraterrestrial spacemen made the maps from space stations in orbit. During one of their visits, they made our ancestors a present of the maps."

Obvious? Well, perhaps not to everyone. Scientists, among others, are skeptical and prefer to look for answers closer to home. However, von Däniken's theories continue to fascinate people, both believers and nonbelievers. And even nonbelievers must admit that space visitors **might have contributed** to human culture. After all, no one can prove that they didn't . . .

Easter Island: Statues of space visitors?

GRAMMAR **PRESENTATION**
SPECULATIONS AND CONCLUSIONS ABOUT THE PAST:
MAY HAVE, MIGHT HAVE, COULD HAVE, MUST HAVE, HAD TO HAVE

STATEMENTS

SUBJECT	MODAL* / HAD TO	HAVE	PAST PARTICIPLE	
They	may (not) might (not) could (not) must (not) had to	have	seen	the statues.

*May, might, could, and must are modals. Modals have only one form. They do not have -s in the third person singular.

CONTRACTIONS

may have	=	may've
might have	=	might've
could have	=	could've
must have	=	must've
could not	=	couldn't

Note: We usually do not contract *may not have, might not have,* and *must not have.*

QUESTIONS

Do / Be	SUBJECT	VERB	
Did	they	carve	these statues?
Were			aliens?

SHORT ANSWERS

SUBJECT	MODAL / HAD TO	HAVE	BEEN
They	may (not) might (not) could (not) must (not) had to	have.	
		have	been.

YES / NO QUESTIONS: COULD

COULD	SUBJECT	HAVE	PAST PARTICIPLE	
Could	he	have	seen	aliens?
			been	an alien?

SHORT ANSWERS

SUBJECT	MODAL / HAD TO	HAVE	BEEN
He	may (not) might (not) could (not) must (not) had to	have.	
		have	been.

WH- QUESTIONS

WH- WORD	COULD	HAVE	PAST PARTICIPLE	
Who	could	have	built	the statues?
What			happened	to these people?

NOTES	EXAMPLES
1. Use *may have*, *might have*, and *could have* to express <u>speculations</u>, or possibilities, about a past situation. These speculations are usually based on facts that we have.	**FACT** Archaeologists found pictures of creatures with wings. **SPECULATIONS** • Space beings **may have visited** that culture. • The pictures **might have marked** a landing strip for a spacecraft. • The pictures **could have shown** mythological creatures.
2. Use *must have* and *had to have* when you are almost certain about your <u>conclusions</u>. USAGE NOTE: We usually do not use *had to have* in negative statements to draw conclusions.	**FACT** The Easter Island statues are made of stone. **CONCLUSIONS** • The islanders **must have had** sharp tools. • The stone **must not have been** too hard for the tools they had. **FACT** The statues are very big. **CONCLUSION** • They **had to have been** difficult to move.
3. *Couldn't have* often expresses a feeling of disbelief or <u>impossibility</u>.	• He **couldn't have drawn** that map! He didn't have enough information.
4. We do not usually use *may have* or *might have* in <u>questions about possibility</u>. We use *could have*.	• **Could** the Nazca people **have drawn** those lines?

5. Use *been* in <u>short answers</u> to questions that include a form of *be*.

> **A:** **Could** von Däniken **have *been*** wrong?
>
> **B:** He certainly **could have *been***. There are other explanations.
>
> **A:** ***Was*** Xesspe surprised when he saw the Nazca lines?
>
> **B:** He **must have *been***. No one knew about them at that time.

However, use only the **modal** + *have* in short answers to <u>questions containing other verbs</u>.

> **A:** **Did** archaeologists **measure** the drawings?
>
> **B:** They ***must have***. They studied them for years.
>
> **A:** **Did** Reis **make** copies of his map?
>
> **B:** He ***might have***. They've found several copies of it already.

---

6. PRONUNCIATION NOTE:
In informal speech, *have* in <u>modal phrases</u> is often pronounced like the word *of*.

> • **could have** /kʊdəv/

▶ **BE CAREFUL!** Do not write *of* instead of *have* with these past modals.

> • They **must *have*** been very skillful.
> Not ~~They must of been . . .~~

REFERENCE NOTE
Could have and *might have* are also used to express past advisability and obligations.
(*See Unit 16.*)

FOCUSED PRACTICE

1 DISCOVER THE GRAMMAR

Match the facts with the conclusions.

Facts

_e_ **1.** The original title of *Chariots of the Gods?* was *Erinnerungen an die Zukunft.*

_a_ **2.** Von Däniken visited every place he described in his book.

_h_ **3.** In 1973, he wrote *In Search of Ancient Gods.*

_c_ **4.** He doesn't have a degree in archaeology.

_f_ **5.** *Chariots of the Gods?* was published the same year as the Apollo moon landing.

_b_ **6.** In the early 1900s, Annie Besant, another writer, said that beings from Venus helped develop culture on Earth.

_d_ **7.** Von Däniken's books sold millions of copies.

_g_ **8.** As soon as von Däniken published his book, scientists attacked him.

Conclusions

a. He must have traveled a lot.

b. He may have known about her ideas.

c. He could have learned about the subject on his own.

d. He must have made a lot of money.

e. He must have written it in German.

f. This scientific achievement must have increased sales of the book.

g. They must not have believed his theories.

h. He might have written other books too.

2 ON THEIR OWN?   Grammar Notes 1–4

Complete the review of Erich von Däniken's book, Chariots of the Gods? *with the verbs in parentheses.*

Who ___could have made___ the Nazca lines? According to Erich von Däniken, author of
              1. (could / make)

this best-seller, ancient human achievements like these present a great mystery. Our ancestors

___couldn't have built___ these structures on their own, he believes. Their cultures were too
2. (could / not build)

primitive. Von Däniken's solution: They ___had to have gotten___ help from space visitors.
                                    3. (had to / get)

Von Däniken's many readers may not realize that practical experiments have helped

explain several of these "mysteries." Von Däniken asks: How ___could___ the

Nazcans ___have planned___ the lines from the ground? Archaeologists now believe that
        4. (could / plan)

this civilization ___might have developed___ flight. They think that ancient Nazcans
              5. (might / develop)

may have drawn pictures of hot-air balloons on pottery. To test their theory,
6. (may / draw)

archaeologists were able to build a similar balloon, using the same material the Nazcans had.

The balloon soared high enough to view the Nazca lines, showing that Nazcans themselves

could have designed the pictures from the air.
7. (could / design)

But what about the Easter Island statues? _Could_ islanders

have cut the huge statues from hard rock with primitive tools? And how
8. (Could / cut)

could only 2,000 people _have moved_ them around the island?
9. (could / move)

When he wrote his book, von Däniken _must have known_ about the Easter Island
10. (must / not know)

experiments of 1955. Working with ancient stone tools, seven Easter Islanders carved the

rough shape of a statue in just three days. Only two hundred men were able to move a

twelve-ton statue across the island. These experiments proved that the ancient islanders

could have carve and _transported_ these statues without any help from
11. (could / carve) 12. (transport)

alien visitors. Not only that, the island's population _might have been_ much larger
13. (might / be)

than von Däniken believes. One scientist speculates that as many as 20,000 people

may have lived on Easter Island.
14. (may / live)

Could space aliens _have helped_ Erich von Däniken write
15. (Could / help)

his book? After all, von Däniken started with no formal education and very little money. How

could he _have visited_ the world's great archaeological sites
16. (could / visit)

and _wrote_ an international best-
17. (write)

seller? Of course, we believe that von Däniken

Could have explored these sites and
18. (could / explore)

developed his ideas without help from
19. (develop)

other worlds. In fact, we give von Däniken a lot more

credit than he gives our ancestors. A wiser response

to the mysterious achievements of the past might be

to say, "Our ancestors _must have had_ great
20. (must / have)

skill, intelligence, and strength to create these

wonderful things."

3 NATURE PUZZLES

Read about these puzzling events and the speculations on their causes. Then rewrite the sentences. Substitute a modal phrase for the underlined words.

Dinosaurs existed on the Earth for about 135 million years. Then, about 65 million years ago, these giant reptiles all died in a short period of time. What could have caused the dinosaurs to become extinct? Here's what scientists say.

1. It's likely that the Earth became colder. (must)

The Earth must have become colder.

2. Probably, dinosaurs didn't survive the cold. (must not)

Dinosaurs must not have survived the cold.

3. It's been suggested that a huge meteor hit the Earth. (might)

A huge meteor might have hit the Earth

4. It's possible that dust from the crash blocked the sun for a long time. (may)

The Dust from the crash may have blocked the sun for a long time.

In 1924, Albert Ostman went camping alone in Canada. Later, he reported that a Bigfoot (a large, hairy creature that looks human) had kidnapped him and taken him home, where the Bigfoot family treated him like a pet. Ostman escaped after several days. What do you think happened? Could a Bigfoot really have kidnapped Ostman?

5. A Bigfoot didn't kidnap Ostman—that's impossible. (couldn't)

A bigfoot couldn't have kidnaped Ostman.

6. Ostman probably saw a bear. (must)

Ostman must have seen a bear.

7. It's possible that Ostman dreamed it. (may)

Ostman may have dreamed it.

8. It could be that he thought his dream was real. (could)

He could have thought his dream was real.

In 1932, a man was taking a walk around Scotland's beautiful Loch Ness. Suddenly, a couple hundred feet from shore, the water bubbled up and a huge monster appeared. The man took a picture. When it was developed, the picture showed something with a long neck and a small head. Since then, many people have reported similar sightings. What do you think? Did the man really see the Loch Ness monster?

9. Most likely the man changed the photograph. (must)

The man must have changed the photograph.

10. Perhaps the man saw a large fish. (might)

The man might have seen a large fish.

11. It's possible that it was a dead tree trunk. (may)

It may have been a dead tree trunk.

12. It's very unlikely that he saw a dinosaur. (couldn't)

He couldn't have seen a dinosaur.

4 ARCHAEOLOGY 101 — Grammar Note 5

Some archaeology students are asking questions in class. Use the modals in parentheses to write short answers.

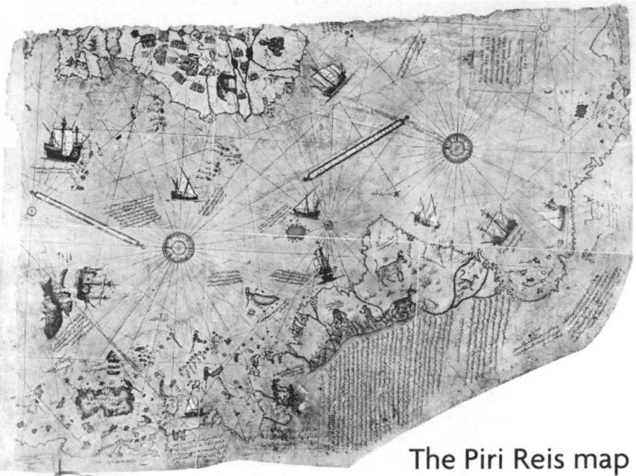

The Piri Reis map

1. A: Do you think the people on Easter Island built the giant statues themselves?

B: They could have. **(could)** They had the knowledge and the tools.

2. A: Were the Nazcans really able to fly?

B: They might have been to. **(might)** There's some evidence that they had hot-air balloons.

3. A: Is it possible that the Nazcan lines were ancient streets?

B: It couldn't have been possible. **(could not)** Some of them just lead to the tops of mountains and then end abruptly. They couldn't have been.

4. A: Do you think the Nazcans used "the streets" during religious ceremonies?

B: They might have. **(might)** But we have no proof.

5. A: Did the sixteenth-century Turkish admiral, Piri Reis, know about Antarctica?

B: He couldn't have known. **(could not)** Antarctica wasn't discovered until 1842.

6. A: Von Däniken says that many ancient artifacts show pictures of astronauts. Could these pictures have illustrated anything closer to Earth?

B: They may have. **(may)** It's possible that the pictures show people dressed in local costumes.

7. A: Was von Däniken upset by all the criticism he received?

B: He might not have been upset. **(might not)** After all, it created more interest in his books.

8. A: Do you think von Däniken helped increase general interest in archaeology?

B: He must have. **(must)** Just look at how many of you are taking this class!

COMMUNICATION PRACTICE

5 LISTENING

Some archaeology students are discussing artifacts they have found at various sites. Look at the pictures. Then listen to the students speculate and draw conclusions about what each item is. Listen again and match the pictures with the appropriate conversation.

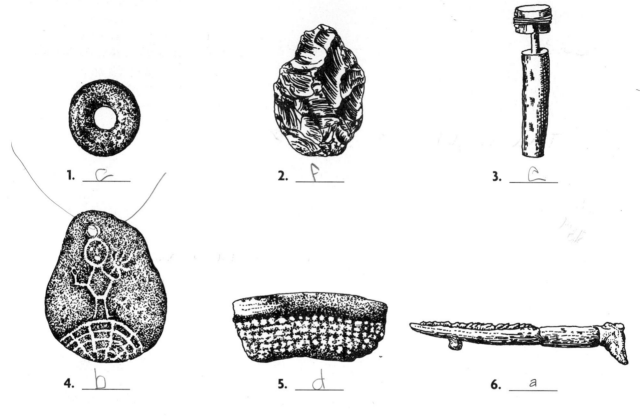

1. c

2. f

3. c

4. b

5. d

6. a

6 USEFUL OBJECTS

Work in small groups. Look at the objects that archaeologists have found in different places. Speculate on what they are and how people might have used them.

1.

Archaeologists found this object in the sleeping area of an ancient Chinese house. It's about the same diameter as a basketball.

EXAMPLE:
I think people might have used this as a foot stool. The floor must have been cold at night, and people could have rested their feet on it.

2.

seguiti a *como*

Archaeologists have found iron objects like these with men's and women's clothing. This one is about the size of a pocket <u>comb</u>.

3.

Objects like these were made of plant fiber or animal skin. They were covered with chalky paste and then painted with figures like these. What could this picture have represented?

4.

This smooth wooden artifact was used by ancient Egyptians. It's about the size of a pencil.

5.

These are made of <u>ivory</u>, and they were found in Alaska. Each one is about the length of a cassette tape. They always come in pairs.

After your discussion, compare your group's ideas with those of the rest of the class.

7 UNSOLVED MYSTERIES

Work in small groups. Read about some famous unsolved mysteries. Speculate on what happened. Think of as many explanations as possible. Then compare your answers with those of another group.

1. The ancient Maya once inhabited the Yucatán Peninsula in what today is Mexico and Guatemala. They had a very advanced civilization. In about A.D. 900, for no known reason, the Maya suddenly left their large and well-built cities. The jungle soon covered the entire area. Why did the Maya abandon their cities? Why did they never return?

   > **EXAMPLE:**
   > Their source of food may have failed. They might have moved to find new food sources.

2. On June 30, 1908, a gigantic object headed toward Earth and exploded in a great ball of fire near the Yenisey River in Siberia. The explosion was one of the strongest ever recorded on Earth. Almost twenty years passed before scientists studied the area. They found miles of burnt land, but absolutely no sign of what had caused the explosion. What could it have been?

3. On October 23, 1947, at about 7:30 A.M. in a small U.S. town, it suddenly started raining fish. The town's bank director reported that hundreds of fish had fallen into his yard, and townspeople were hit by the falling fish as they walked to work. The fish were only the kinds found in local rivers and lakes, and they were all very fresh. Nothing else—no frogs, turtles, or water plants—fell that morning, only fish. How could this have happened?

8 CHARIOTS OF THE GODS?

Reread the article that begins on page 249. Then discuss your opinion about Erich von Däniken's theory with a partner. Afterward, have a class discussion. How many students think space creatures might have visited the Earth? How many think space creatures couldn't have affected human culture?

9 WRITING

Read the following information about an archeological discovery. Then write a paragraph in which you speculate who the Ice Man was and what happened to him.

In 1991, hikers in the Italian Alps discovered a body in some melting ice. The body, which had been in the ice for more than 5,000 years, was in almost perfect condition. The "Ice Man" had several broken ribs. He had been wearing warm winter clothing, and had been carrying a knife, an ax, dried meat, and medicines. He had been making a bow and arrows, but he had not finished them. At the time he lived, people had already started to live in villages, to farm, and to keep animals. They brought their animals high into the mountains to feed. Other tribes sometimes attacked villages.

REVIEW OR SELFTEST

PART

VII

I. *Complete the conversation by circling the correct modals.*

A: You <u>should have / (must have)</u> been up late last night. You look tired.
1.

B: I <u>couldn't / didn't have to</u> sleep. My boss passed me up for a raise. He
2.

<u>could have / couldn't have</u> given me one. I've been there a whole year.
3.

A: I <u>can't / don't have to</u> believe he did that! Well, the company
4.

<u>could / must not</u> have the money right now.
5.

B: Wrong. Ann got a raise and a promotion. And she<u>'s got to / should</u> be the
6.

worst employee there. By the way, your friend Amy also got a promotion.

A: Really? She <u>has to / may</u> be pleased about that. But, getting back to you—
7.

you <u>should / shouldn't</u> call me when you get upset. I
8.

<u>must have / might have</u> been able to help last night.
9.

B: I did call you. You <u>must have / might not have</u> been out.
10.

A: I wasn't out. I <u>could not have / must not have</u> heard the phone. I
11.

<u>could have / ought to have</u> been in the shower.
12.

B: Well, I ended up calling Sam. What a mistake. I <u>should / shouldn't have</u>
13.

called him. He repeated everything to Ann.

A: That's terrible! He <u>ought not to have / must not have</u> done that. I'm going
14.

to talk with him about it.

B: You <u>couldn't / 'd better not</u>. He'll just repeat that conversation, too.
15.

II. *Complete the conversation with past modals. Use the correct forms of the verbs in parentheses. Choose between affirmative and negative.*

A: I got a C on my math test. I ___should have done___ better than that.
1. (should / do)

B: Don't be so hard on yourself. It ___may not have been___ your fault. It just
2. (may / be)

___could have been___ a more difficult test than usual.
3. (could / be)

(continued on next page)

A: No, it ___couldn't have been___ that difficult. The rest of the class did pretty well.
4. (could / be)

I ___should have studied___ harder.
5. (should / study)

B: What ___could have___ you ___have done___ differently?
6. (could / do)

A: Well, for one thing, I ___shouldn't have miss___ that day of class.
7. (should / miss)

B: You missed a day? Did you get the notes?

A: No. I ___ought not to have copied___ them. Some of the problems I got wrong
8. (ought to / copy)

___must have came___ from that day.
9. (must / come)

III. *Summarize these sentences. Use the past form of the modals in parentheses. Choose between affirmative and negative.*

1. It was a mistake to stay up so late.

   (should) ___I shouldn't have stayed up so late.___

2. I regret not watching the show about von Däniken.

   (should) _____

3. I'm sure it was very interesting.

   (must) ___I'm sure it must have been very interesting___

4. I was surprised that the local library never bought his books.

   (ought to) _____

5. I'm annoyed at Sara for not reminding me about it.

   (should) _____

6. I wish that John had told me about it.

   (could) _____

7. I'm sure he didn't remember our conversation about it.

   (must) _____

8. I feel bad that my roommate didn't invite me to the party.

   (might) _____

9. It's possible that John didn't get an invitation.

   (might) _____

10. I'm sure he didn't forget our date.

    (could) _____

IV. *Circle the letter of the correct word or words to complete each sentence.*

1. There are no clean socks. I should _____ the laundry yesterday.   A B (C) D
   (A) did   (C) have done
   (B) do   (D) not have done

2. Kai wants better grades next semester. He _____ harder.   A (B) C D
   (A) must have studied   (C) must not study
   (B) will have to study   (D) shouldn't study

3. Dana didn't buy her brother a birthday card. She must _____.   (A) B C D
   (A) have forgotten   (C) forget
   (B) not have forgotten   (D) forgets

4. My wallet is missing. I _____ dropped it in the store.   A B C D
   (A) ought to have   (C) could have
   (B) might   (D) must

5. He's going for a walk in a few minutes. He may _____ at Molly's   A B C (D)
   on the way.
   (A) have stopped   (C) stops
   (B) stopping   (D) stop

6. You're not coming tonight? It's already seven o'clock! You _____   A (B) C D
   let me know sooner.
   (A) may   (C) can't
   (B) might have   (D) must have

7. You should _____ "The Simpsons" tomorrow night. I hear that   A B (C) D
   it's going to be a really funny show.
   (A) have missed   (C) not miss
   (B) not have missed   (D) miss

8. Mayan buildings are beautiful. The Mayans must _____ an   A (B) C D
   advanced civilization.
   (A) have   (C) had
   (B) have had   (D) had had

9. I don't understand this show. Clio was in Tampa on Thursday, so she   A B (C) D
   couldn't _____ the money from a Boston bank that day.
   (A) steal   (C) have stolen
   (B) had stolen   (D) stole

10. I'm sorry, but I _____ able to meet you for lunch tomorrow.   (A) B C D
    (A) won't be   (C) can't be
    (B) haven't been   (D) don't be

V. *Read this journal entry. There are nine mistakes in the use of modals. Find and correct them. The first mistake is already corrected.*

Friday, October 25

What a day! I guess I'd ~~not better~~ better not stay up so late anymore.

This morning I should of gotten up much earlier. When I got

to the post office, the lines were already long. I must have

wait at least half an hour. My boss was furious that I was

late. He might fires me for lateness—even though I couldn't

have worked in that time anyway! The computers were down

again. We must had lost four hours that way. While the

system was down, some of us were able go out to lunch. Later,

we all felt sick. It had to has been the food—we all ate the

same thing. On the way home, I got stuck in traffic. A trip

that should taken twenty minutes took forty-five. Tomorrow's

Saturday. I just might sleeping until noon.

▶ *To check your answers, go to the Answer Key on page 268.*

From Grammar to Writing Organizing Ideas from Freewriting

Freewriting is a way to develop ideas about a topic. To freewrite, write for a specified length of time without stopping. Do not worry about mistakes. Then organize the ideas in your freewriting.

 Read Clara's freewriting about a problem she had with her cousin Miguel. Underline her ideas about Miguel's reasons for what he did. Bracket ([ ]) her ideas about the appropriateness of Miguel's and her own behavior.

> Can't stop thinking about Miguel's wedding in Quito last year. Still feeling hurt and confused. Why didn't he invite me? Or even tell me about it? [This was a family reunion and he should have sent everyone an invitation.] He knows I'm a student, and <u>he must have thought I couldn't afford the airfare to Ecuador.</u> He could've sent me an invitation and let me decide for myself. On the other hand, I should have called him to discuss it. He might have even decided that I couldn't afford to send a gift. He shouldn't have decided for me. He couldn't have been angry with me! I've got to let him know how I feel. I should write a letter.

2 *Clara decided to write a letter to Miguel. Read the outline for her letter in Exercise 3. In which paragraph does Clara . . . ?*

a. discuss the appropriateness of Miguel's and her own behavior ___3___

b. introduce the problem _____

c. suggest resolving the problem _____

d. speculate on reasons for Miguel's behavior _____

3 *Complete Clara's letter with ideas from the freewriting in Exercise 1.*

Dear Miguel,

I'm sorry that I haven't written for some time, but I'm still feeling hurt and confused. Miguel, why didn't you invite me to your wedding last year? You didn't even tell me about it!

Maybe your reasons for not inviting me were actually thoughtful. You know I'm a student, and ___you must have thought I couldn't afford the airfare.___

_____

_____

_____

However, I believe you should have handled the situation in a different way. This was a family reunion, and you should have sent everyone an invitation.

_____

_____

_____

We ought to solve this as soon as possible. I miss you. Please write as soon as you get this letter.

Clara

4 *Before you write . . .*

- Think of a problem you had with a friend or relative. Freewrite about the problem: the reasons it might have happened and what you and other people could have done differently.

- Choose ideas and organize them. Then write a letter.

- Use past modals to speculate about reasons for your problem and to express regrets and obligations.

5 *Exchange letters with a partner. Answer the following questions. Put a question mark (?) over anything in the letter that seems wrong.*

  a. Did the writer correctly use past modals to speculate on reasons?   Yes / No

  b. Did the write correctly use past modals to express appropriateness?   Yes / No

  c. Did the writer express his or her feelings and ideas clearly?   Yes / No

6 *Revise your letter. Make any necessary corrections.*

I. **(Units 15–17)**

2. couldn't
3. could have
4. can't
5. must not
6. 's got to
7. has to
8. should
9. might have
10. must have
11. must not have
12. could have
13. shouldn't have
14. ought not to have
15. 'd better not

II. **(Units 15–17)**

2. may not have been
3. could have been
4. couldn't have been
5. should have studied
6. could . . . have done
7. shouldn't have missed
8. ought to have copied
9. must have come

III. **(Units 15–17)**

2. I should've watched the show about von Däniken.
3. It must've been very interesting.
4. The local library ought to have bought his books.
5. Sara should've reminded me about it.
6. John could've told me about it.
7. He must not have remembered our conversation about it.
8. My roommate might've invited me to the party.
9. John might not have gotten an invitation.
10. He couldn't have forgotten our date.

IV. **(Units 15–17)**

2. B   7. C
3. A   8. B
4. C   9. C
5. D   10. A
6. B

V. **(Units 15–17)**

What a day! I guess I'd ~~not better~~ *better not*

stay up so late anymore. This morning
I should ~~of~~ *have* gotten up much earlier.

When I got to the post office, the lines
were already long. I must have ~~wait~~ *waited* at

least half an hour. My boss was

furious that I was late. He might ~~fires~~ *fire*

me for lateness—even though I

couldn't have worked in that time

anyway! The computers were down

again. We must ~~had~~ *have* lost four hours

that way. While the system was down,
some of us were able ∧*to* go out to lunch.

Later, we all felt sick. It had to ~~has~~ *have*

been the food—we all ate the same

thing. On the way home, I got stuck in
traffic. A trip that should ∧*have* taken twenty

minutes took forty-five. Tomorrow's
Saturday. I just might ~~sleeping~~ *sleep* until

noon.

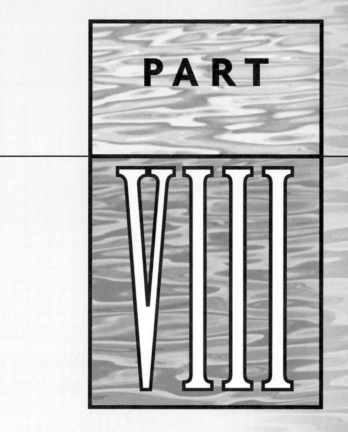

PART

VIII

THE PASSIVE

THE PASSIVE: OVERVIEW

GRAMMAR **IN CONTEXT**

BEFORE YOU READ Look at the ad. What are the people reading? What do you know about this magazine? What kinds of magazines do you enjoy?

Read this advertisement for "the world's most widely read magazine."

The World Keeps Informed With Reader's Digest

Reader's Digest
We make a difference in 100 million lives worldwide.

Reader's Digest **was founded** in 1922. Today it **is read** by people in every country in the world. It **is published** in nineteen languages and forty-eight editions. Each foreign-language edition **is** especially **tailored** to fit the needs and interests of its international audience. Last year *Reader's Digest* **was read** by 100 million people. Shouldn't you be one of them? Subscribe today.

GRAMMAR **PRESENTATION**
THE PASSIVE

ACTIVE	PASSIVE
Millions of people **buy** it.	It **is bought** by millions of people.
Someone **published** it in 1922.	It **was published** in 1922.

PASSIVE STATEMENTS

SUBJECT	BE *(NOT)*	PAST PARTICIPLE	*(BY* + OBJECT)	
It	**is (not)**	**bought**	by millions of people.	
It	**was (not)**	**published**		in 1922.

YES / NO QUESTIONS

BE	SUBJECT	PAST PARTICIPLE	
Is **Was**	it	**sold**	in Ukraine?

SHORT ANSWERS

	AFFIRMATIVE	
Yes,	it	**is.** **was.**

SHORT ANSWERS

	NEGATIVE	
No,	it	**isn't.** **wasn't.**

WH- QUESTIONS

WH- WORD	BE	SUBJECT	PAST PARTICIPLE
Where	**is** **was**	it	**sold**?

NOTES	EXAMPLES
1. Active and **passive sentences** often have similar meanings, but a <u>different focus</u>.	**ACTIVE** • Millions of people **read** the magazine. *(The focus is on the people.)* **PASSIVE** • The magazine **is read** by millions of people. *(The focus is on the magazine.)*
2. Form the **passive** with a form of **be** + **past participle**.	• It **is written** in nineteen different languages. • It **was published** in 1922.
3. Use the passive in the following situations: **a.** When the <u>agent</u> (the person or thing doing the action) is <u>unknown or not important</u>. **b.** When the identity of the <u>agent is clear from the context</u>. **c.** When you want to <u>avoid mentioning the agent</u>.	• The magazine **was founded** in 1922. *(I don't know who founded it.)* • The magazine **is sold** at newsstands. *(We can assume that the newsstand owners and employees sell it. It is not necessary to mention them.)* • Some mistakes **were made** in that article on Bolivia. *(I know who made the mistakes, but I don't want to blame the person who made them.)*

4. Use the **passive with** *by* if you <u>mention the agent</u>. Mention the agent in the following situations:

- **a.** when you introduce <u>necessary new information about the agent</u>.

  - The article **was written** *by a psychologist*.

  - John Delgado is a famous sports writer. Recently, he **was hired** *by International Sports* to write a monthly column.
  (The name of John's employer is necessary new information.)

- **b.** when you want to give credit to someone who <u>created something</u>.

  - The soccer article **was written** *by John Delgado*.
  - The cotton gin **was invented** *by Eli Whitney*.

- **c.** when the agent is <u>surprising</u>.

  - Our windows **are washed** *by a robot*.

▶ **BE CAREFUL!** In most cases, you do not need to mention an agent in passive sentences. Do not include an agent unnecessarily.

  - John Delgado completed a good soccer article recently. It **was written** last month, but it won't appear until next spring.
  NOT It was written last month ~~by him~~ . . . .

FOCUSED PRACTICE

1 DISCOVER THE GRAMMAR

Read the sentences and decide if they are **Active (A)** *or* **Passive (P)**.

___P___ 1. *Reader's Digest* was founded in 1922.

_____ 2. It was founded by DeWitt Wallace and Lila Acheson Wallace.

_____ 3. Millions of people read it.

_____ 4. It is translated into many other languages.

_____ 5. A large-type edition is also printed.

_____ 6. It is also recorded.

_____ 7. Proofreaders are hired to correct mistakes.

_____ 8. They look for mistakes in spelling and grammar.

_____ 9. *Reader's Digest* is sold at newsstands.

_____ 10. It is published once a month.

_____ 11. Many of the articles are condensed from other sources.

_____ 12. Many readers subscribe to *Reader's Digest*.

_____ 13. I bought a copy last week.

_____ 14. One of the articles was written by a famous scientist.

_____ 15. It was translated from Spanish into English.

2 MANY TONGUES   Grammar Notes 1–3

Look at the chart. Then complete the sentences. Decide between the active and passive.

Language	Number of Speakers (in Millions)
Arabic	246
Cantonese (China)	71
English	508
Ho (Bihar and Orissa States, India)	1
Japanese	126
Spanish	417
Swahili (Kenya, Tanzania, Uganda, Democratic Republic of Congo)	49
Tagalog (Philippines)	57

Source: The World Almanac and Book of Facts 1999 (N.J., 1998).

1. Japanese ___is spoken by 126 million people___.

2. One million people _____.

3. _____ by 57 million people.

4. Spanish_____.

5. _____ Cantonese.

6. _____ 246 million people.

7. More than 500 million people _____.

8. _____ in Uganda.

---

3 AN INTERVIEW   **Grammar Note 2**

Jill Jones is writing an article about Bolivia. Use the passive form of the verbs in parentheses and short answers to complete her interview with a Bolivian cultural attaché.

JONES: I'm writing an article about Bolivia, and I'd like to check my information.

ATTACHÉ: Certainly. How can I help you?

JONES: First, I'd like to find out about the early history of Bolivia. _____Was_____

the area first ____inhabited____ by the Inca?
                    1. (inhabit)

ATTACHÉ: _____. There was a great civilization on the shores of Lake Titicaca
              2.

long before the Inca flourished. That civilization _____ probably

_____ by ancestors of the Aymara, who still live in Bolivia.
    3. (create)

JONES: That's fascinating. Changing the topic, though, let me ask about the agriculture

of your country. I know potatoes are an important crop in the mountains.

_____ corn _____ in the Andes as well?
                              4. (grow)

ATTACHÉ: _____. The climate is too cold and dry. But quinoa is. Quinoa is a
              5.

traditional grain that grows well in the mountains.

JONES: Quinoa? How _____ that _____, with a *k*?
                                              6. (spell)

ATTACHÉ: No, with a *q*—q-u-i-n-o-a.

JONES: OK. Thanks. Now, I know our readers will want to read about llamas. How

_____ they _____?
                    7. (use)

(continued on next page)

ATTACHÉ: They have many uses—fur, meat, transportation. But only in the highlands.

JONES: Really? Why _____ they _____ there and not in

8. (raise)

the lowlands?

ATTACHÉ: They're suited to the mountain climate and terrain. They don't do well in

the lowlands.

JONES: I see. I understand that tin is an important resource. Where _____

it _____?

9. (mine)

ATTACHÉ: The richest deposits are in the Andes.

JONES: Let's talk about some other resources. How about the eastern part of the

country—the Oriente. What crops _____ there?

10. (grow)

ATTACHÉ: The most important crop is rice. We also raise cattle there.

JONES: Are there any other natural resources in the lowlands?

ATTACHÉ: Yes. Oil. Petroleum _____ there.

11. (find)

JONES: OK, let's talk about languages for a moment. I know that Spanish is the official

language of Bolivia. But _____ any other languages

_____?

12. (speak)

ATTACHÉ: _____. Actually, more people speak Native American languages

_13._

than Spanish—especially Quechua and Aymara.

JONES: I've heard that naturalists love to visit Bolivia. _____ condors still

_____ in the mountains?

14. (see)

ATTACHÉ: _____. They live in the highest regions. And in the rain forests

_15._

there are a lot of fascinating animals—parrots, boa constrictors, jaguars—many,

many species.

JONES: Well, thank you very much. You've been really helpful. By the way, I'm planning

to visit La Paz next month. I've heard that Bolivian textiles are very beautiful.

ATTACHÉ: Yes, that's true. They _____ still _____ by hand. And

16. (make)

be sure to listen to some traditional music, too.

4 CHANGES

There were a lot of changes at Modern Reader *magazine this year. Read the notes for an article for the employee newsletter and then complete the article. Use the passive form of the words in the box.*

Last Year	This Year
20 employees	40 employees
10 computers	20 computers
one floor	two floors
English only	English, Spanish, and Japanese
print and recorded editions	print only
John Crandon, managing editor	Nora Gilbert, managing editor
hours: 9:00–6:00	hours: 9:00–5:00
vacation: 10 days	vacation: 14 days

appreciate   build   buy   discontinue   ~~hire~~   increase   publish   reduce   replace

We have many exciting changes to celebrate at *Modern Reader* this year. During the year, twenty new employees ____were hired____, and ten new computers _____ for
1.   2.
the new staff. Of course, this meant we needed more room, so in July, new offices

_____ for us on the second floor.
3.

What started this growth spurt? Partly the success of *Modern Reader* with English-

speaking readers, and partly our new foreign-language editions. As most of you know, our

first Spanish and Japanese editions of *Modern Reader* _____ this year, and
4.

they have already found a large audience. Unfortunately, our recorded edition

_____ last month because of lack of interest.
5.

In November, we were sad to say goodbye to John Crandon, who decided to retire. In

December, John _____ by Nora Gilbert, our new managing editor.
6.

Finally, some changes in our workday. Working hours _____, and vacation
7.

days _____ this year.
8.

I know these changes _____ by our families, who got to see us more. We
9.

look forward to seeing what exciting changes next year will bring.

5 **CHECKING FACTS**

Jill Jones's editor found and circled nine factual mistakes in this article. On the next page, rewrite the incorrect sentences with information from Exercise 3. Use the passive in each pair of sentences.

A Land of Contrasts
by Jill Jones

Visitors to Bolivia are amazed by the contrasts and charmed by the beauty of this South American country's landscapes—from the breathtaking Andes in the west to the tropical lowlands in the east.

Two-thirds of Bolivia's five million people are concentrated in the cool western highlands or Altiplano. Today, as in centuries past, (corn) and (kuinoa) *spelling?* are grown in the mountains. Llamas are raised only for (transportation). And tin, Bolivia's richest natural resource, is mined in the high Andes.

The Oriente, another name for the eastern lowlands, is mostly tropical. Rice is the major food crop, and (llamas) are raised for meat in the lowlands. (Rubber) is also found in this region.

Bolivia is home to many fascinating forms of wildlife. The colorful (parrot) is seen in the highest mountains. Boa constrictors, jaguars, and many other animals are found in the rain forests.

Hundreds of years before the Inca flourished, a great civilization was created on the shores of (the Pacific), probably by ancestors of Bolivia's Aymara people. Their descendants still speak the Aymara language. Today, Native American languages are still widely spoken in Bolivia. Although (Portuguese) is spoken in the government, Quechua and Aymara are used more widely by the people.

Traditional textiles are woven by (machine). Music is played on reed pipes whose tone resembles the sound of the wind blowing over high plains in the Andes.

1. _Corn isn't grown in the mountains. Potatoes are grown in the mountains._

2. _____

3. _____

4. _____

5. _____

6. _____

7. _____

8. _____

9. _____

6 DID YOU KNOW?   **Grammar Notes 3 and 4**

John Delgado wrote a soccer trivia column for International Sports. *Complete the information with the correct form of the verbs in the first set of parentheses. Only include the agent (from the second set of parentheses) if absolutely necessary.*

• Soccer is the most popular sport in the world. It _is played by more than 20 million people_ .
  1. (play) (more than 20 million people)

• It _____ is called _____ football _____ in 144 countries.
  2. (call)   ~~people~~

• Except for the goalie, players _____ to use their hands.
  3. (not allow) (the rules)

  Instead, the ball _____ .
  4. (control) (the feet, the head, and the body)

• Soccer _____ in the United States very much until
  5. (not play) (people)

  twenty years ago. The game _____ in the 1970s.
  6. (make popular) (Pelé and other international stars)

• Soccer has a long history. A form of soccer _____ in
  7. (enjoy) (Chinese people)

  China 2,000 years ago.

• It _____ in 1365—his archers spent too much time
  8. (ban) (King Edward III of England)

  playing, and too little time practicing archery.

• Medieval games _____ for entire days, over miles
  9. (play) (players)

  of territory.

• Today, the World Cup games _____ every four years.
  10. (hold) (The World Cup Association)

  The best teams in the world compete.

COMMUNICATION PRACTICE

7 LISTENING

Listen to the conversations between editors at Modern Reader. *Then listen again and circle the letter of the sentence you hear from each pair.*

1. **a.** Jill hired Bob.
   b. Jill was hired by Bob.

2. **a.** I trained Minna.
   b. I was trained by Minna.

3. **a.** It's published just six times a year.
   b. It was published just six times a year.

4. **a.** Tony fired Jill.
   b. Tony was fired by Jill.

5. **a.** She interviewed Jay.
   b. She was interviewed by Jay.

6. **a.** He was laid off.
   b. Was he laid off?

8 TRANSLATIONS

These are some non-English titles of Reader's Digest.* *Work in small groups. Try to guess which language each title is written in and where it is sold.*

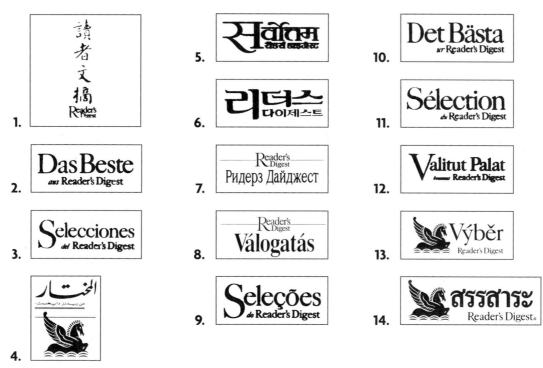

1. 讀者文摘 Reader's Digest
2. Das Beste aus Reader's Digest
3. Selecciones del Reader's Digest
4. المختار
5. सर्वोत्तम
6. 리더스 다이제스트
7. Reader's Digest Ридерз Дайджест
8. Reader's Digest Válogatás
9. Seleções do Reader's Digest
10. Det Bästa ur Reader's Digest
11. Sélection du Reader's Digest
12. Valitut Palat Reader's Digest
13. Výběr Reader's Digest
14. สรรสาระ Reader's Digest

*Reprinted with permission of The Reader's Digest Association, Inc.

EXAMPLE:

A: I think Number 2 is written in German.

B: Right. And it's probably sold in Germany and Austria.

C: It's probably also sold in Switzerland.

9 INFORMATION GAP: THE PHILIPPINES

The Philippines consist of many islands. The two largest are Luzon in the north and Mindanao in the south.

Work in pairs (A and B). You and your partner will be looking at different maps. The maps show some of the many important products found and made in the Philippines. Your task is to find out about each other's maps.

Student B, look at the Information Gap on page 284 and follow the instructions there.

*Student A, look at the map of Luzon below. Complete the chart for Luzon. Write **Y** for **Yes** and **N** for **No**. Ask Student B questions about Mindanao and complete the chart for Mindanao. Answer Student B's questions about Luzon.*

EXAMPLE:

A: Is tobacco grown in Mindanao?

B: No, it isn't.
Is it grown in Luzon?

A: Yes, it is. It's grown in the north and central part of the island.

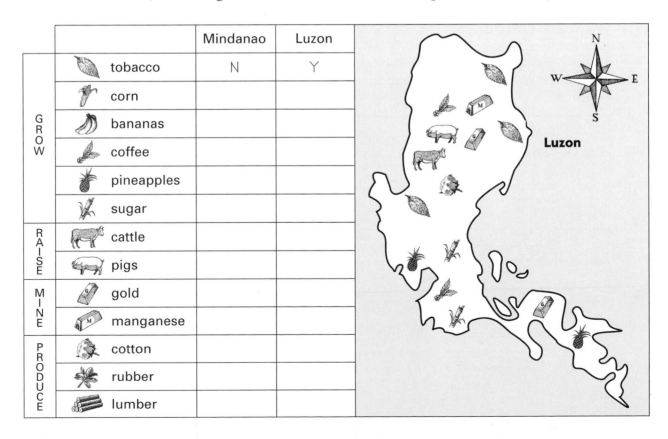

		Mindanao	Luzon
GROW	tobacco	N	Y
	corn		
	bananas		
	coffee		
	pineapples		
	sugar		
RAISE	cattle		
	pigs		
MINE	gold		
	manganese		
PRODUCE	cotton		
	rubber		
	lumber		

When you are done, compare charts. Are they the same?

10 TRIVIA QUIZ

Magazines often have games and puzzles. Work in pairs. Complete this quiz. Then compare your answers with those of your classmates.

Do you know . . . ?

1. Urdu is spoken in _____.
   a. Ethiopia   **b.** Pakistan   **c.** Uruguay

2. Air conditioning was invented in _____.
   a. 1902   **b.** 1950   **c.** 1980

3. The X-ray was discovered by _____.
   a. Thomas Edison   **b.** Wilhelm Roentgen   **c.** Marie Curie

4. The World Trade Center in New York was designed by _____.
   a. Minoru Yamasaki   **b.** Frank Lloyd Wright   **c.** I. M. Pei

5. The 1988 Summer Olympics were held in _____.
   a. Germany   **b.** Japan   **c.** South Korea

6. A baby _____ is called a cub.
   a. cat   **b.** dog   **c.** lion

Now, with your partner, make up your own questions with the words in parentheses. For item 10, add your own question. Ask another pair to answer your questions.

7. _____ _____ by _____.
                              (paint)
   a. _____ **b.** _____ **c.** _____

8. _____ _____ by _____.
                              (invent)
   a. _____ **b.** _____ **c.** _____

9. _____ _____ by _____.
                              (compose)
   a. _____ **b.** _____ **c.** _____

10. _____ _____ by _____.
   a. _____ **b.** _____ **c.** _____

11 SAID AROUND THE WORLD

Reader's Digest *often has a page of famous quotations or sayings like these. What do you think they mean? Discuss them in small groups.*

Rome wasn't built in a day. *(English)*

He who was bitten by a snake avoids tall grass. *(Chinese)*

As fast as laws are devised their evasion is contrived. *(German)*

The torch of love is lit in the kitchen. *(French)*

He ran away from the rain and was caught in a hailstorm. *(Turkish)*

The stitch is lost unless the thread is knotted. *(Italian)*

Never promise a fish until it's caught. *(Irish)*

12 WRITING

Complete the table with information about a country that you know well. Then write an essay about the country, using the information you have gathered. Use the article in Exercise 5 as a model.

Name of country	
Geographical areas	
Crops grown in each area	
Animals raised in each area	
Natural resources found in each area	
Wildlife found in each area	
Languages spoken	
Art, handicrafts, or music created	

INFORMATION GAP FOR STUDENT B

Student B, look at the map of Mindanao. Complete the chart for Mindanao. Write
Y *for* **Yes** *and* **N** *for* **No**. *Answer Student A's questions about Mindanao. Ask*
Student A questions about Luzon and complete the chart for Luzon.

EXAMPLE:

A: Is tobacco grown in Mindanao?

B: No, it isn't.
Is it grown in Luzon?

A: Yes, it is. It's grown in the north and central part of the island.

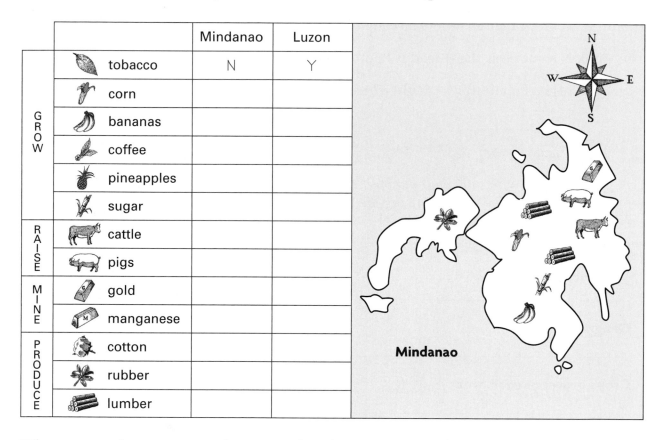

			Mindanao	Luzon	
G R O W		tobacco	N	Y	
		corn			
		bananas			
		coffee			
		pineapples			
		sugar			
R A I S E		cattle			
		pigs			
M I N E		gold			
		manganese			
P R O D U C E		cotton			
		rubber			
		lumber			

Mindanao

When you are done, compare charts. Are they the same?

THE PASSIVE WITH MODALS AND MODAL-LIKE EXPRESSIONS

GRAMMAR **IN CONTEXT**

BEFORE YOU READ What does the title of the article mean? What are some problems that can occur when people from different cultures must live and work together?

Read this article about an international space project.

CloseQuarters

Japanese astronauts fear that decisions **will be made** too fast, while Americans worry that in an emergency, they **might not be made** quickly enough. The French and Dutch worry that dinner **won't be taken** seriously, and Italians suspect that their privacy **may not be respected**.

The focus of all this apprehension is the space station *Unity*, a major international project that was launched in 1998. Within the next few years, *Unity* **will be operated** by a crew of astronauts from Europe, Japan, Canada, Russia, and the United States. At first, the crew **will be replaced** every ninety days, but the stay **could be lengthened** to prepare for a two-year trip to Mars.

How **can** an international group of astronauts **be expected** to get along during long periods in this "trapped environment"?

To find out, anthropologist Mary Lozano and engineer Clifford Wong asked astronauts from around the world about their concerns. The two scientists are hopeful that many cross-cultural problems **will be avoided** by what they have learned.

(continued on next page)

(Bottom to top) Canadian astronaut Julie Payette, U.S. astronaut Tamara Jernigan, and Russian cosmonaut Valery Tokarev in the International Space Station's *Unity* module.

CloseQuarters (continued)

Besides the concerns already mentioned, all the astronauts worry about language. English will be the official language of the station, and, of course, a great deal of technical language **must be mastered** by everyone. However, on a social level, some partners fear that they **might be treated** like outsiders because they won't know American slang. Another concern is food. What time **should** meals **be served**? How **should** preparation and cleanup **be handled**? **Can** religious dietary restrictions **be observed** on board?

The International Space Station *Unity* being assembled in space.

To deal with cross-cultural differences like these, Lozano and Wong feel strongly that astronauts **should be taught** interpersonal skills as well as **given** technical and survival know-how. They have interviewed participants in each country, and they hope that what they learn from them **will be applied** in training. In the long run, they believe, cross-cultural training will save money and reduce errors caused by misunderstanding, ranging from misreading a facial expression to incorrectly interpreting data.

Often qualities like sensitivity and tolerance **can't be taught** from a textbook; they **have to be observed** and **experienced**. Lozano and Wong say that the necessary model for space station harmony **can be found** in the TV series *Star Trek*. The multicultural *Enterprise* crew has been getting along in space for eons now, and the scientists suggest that watching the show might be helpful for future astronauts. Since cross-cultural harmony **could be imagined** by the *Star Trek* creators, it **can be achieved** by the crew of *Unity*. This might turn out to be the project's greatest achievement.

—LISA DOBRUS

Source: Based on information from Judith Stone, "It's a Small World after All," *Discover* magazine, (February 1992) pp. 23–25.

GRAMMAR **PRESENTATION**
THE PASSIVE WITH MODALS AND MODAL-LIKE EXPRESSIONS

			STATEMENTS	
SUBJECT	MODAL*	BE	PAST PARTICIPLE	
The crew	will (not) should (not) must (not) can (not) had better (not)	be	replaced	next month.

* Modals have only one form. They do not have -s in the third-person singular.

			STATEMENTS	
SUBJECT	HAVE (GOT) TO / BE GOING TO	BE	PAST PARTICIPLE	
The crew	has (got) to doesn't have to is (not) going to	be	replaced	next month.

	YES / NO QUESTIONS				SHORT ANSWERS			SHORT ANSWERS	
MODAL	SUBJECT	BE	PAST PARTICIPLE		AFFIRMATIVE			NEGATIVE	
Will	it	be	replaced?		Yes, it	will.		No, it	won't.
Should						should.			shouldn't.
Must						must.			must not.
Can						can.			can't.

	YES / NO QUESTIONS				SHORT ANSWERS		SHORT ANSWERS	
AUXILIARY VERB	SUBJECT	HAVE TO / GOING TO	BE	PAST PARTICIPLE	AFFIRMATIVE		NEGATIVE	
Does	it	have to	be	replaced?	Yes, it	does.	No, it	doesn't.
Is		going to				is.		isn't.

NOTES	**EXAMPLES**
1. After a modal, form the passive with <u>base form of *be*</u> + **past participle**.	• The shuttle *will* **be used** to launch the space station. • The launch *won't* **be postponed**. • The crew *must* **be given** time off. • Decisions *shouldn't* **be made** too quickly.
2. Use *will* or *be going to* with the passive to talk about the **future**.	• It *will* **be launched** very soon. <div align="center">OR</div>• It*'s going to* **be launched** very soon.
3. Use *can* with the passive to express **present ability**. Use *could* with the passive to express **past ability**.	• The blastoff *can* **be seen** for miles. • It *could* **be seen** very clearly last year.
4. Use *could*, *may*, *might*, and *can't* with the passive to express **future possibility** or **impossibility**.	• It *could* **be launched** very soon. • French scientists *may* **be invited** to participate. • Plants *might* **be grown** on board. • It *can't* **be done**.
5. Use *have (got) to*, *had better*, *should*, *ought to*, and *must* with the passive to express **a.** advisability **b.** obligation **c.** necessity *(To review modals and modal-like verbs, see Unit 15.)*	 • The crew *should* **be prepared** to deal with cultural differences. • Crew members *ought to* **be given** communication training. • Privacy *had better* **be respected**. • Everyone *must* **be consulted**.

FOCUSED PRACTICE

1 DISCOVER THE GRAMMAR

Read this article about comfort in space. Underline all the examples of the passive with modals and modal-like expressions.

A Comfortable Space

Ten former astronauts were recently asked about what <u>could be done</u> to improve comfort in space. Here are some of the issues they raised.

• **FOOD** Wherever you are, mealtime is important for your sense of well-being. The astronauts feel they should be able to enjoy what they eat, but food just doesn't taste good in zero gravity. This problem can be overcome by making the food spicier. A little pepper or mustard could go a long way in making meals more palatable.

• **CLOTHING** The temperature on board a space station can vary from one part to the other. To stay comfortable, the astronauts suggested layered garments. The top layer could be removed in warmer sections of the station. Astronauts could also be provided with different uniforms for different occasions. Having a choice of style and color might boost morale.

• **PRIVACY** Living in tight quarters doesn't allow for much privacy. All agreed that this might pose a serious problem on long trips. No one had any answers, but they felt strongly that solutions to this issue should be investigated.

• **SLEEPING** Because of weightlessness and other factors, sleep is often interrupted in space. One astronaut feared that there might be long-term effects as a result of never getting a good night's rest.

• **DEATH** No one likes to think about this issue, but it is possible that an astronaut could die while aboard the space station. What should be done if this happens? One astronaut suggested that the body could be frozen and then brought back to Earth.

• **EMOTIONAL NEEDS** Many of the astronauts pointed out that people have the same needs in space as they do on Earth. They believe that time should be provided for relaxation, and that everything possible ought to be done to make the astronauts feel happy and at home.

Source: Based on information from William K. Douglas, *Human Performance Issues Arising from Manned Space Station Missions* (prepared for Ames Research Center, National Aeronautics and Space Administration, 1986).

2 ZERO-G

Complete this interview between Comet Magazine (CM) *and aerospace engineer Dr. Bernard Kay.*

CM: Dr. Kay, I'd like to ask how daily life <u>will be conducted</u> in a space station.
1. (will / conduct)

DR. KAY: Sure. What would you like to know?

CM: First, about food. _____ it _____ on board or
2. (Will / prepare)

_____ out of tubes?
3. (squeeze)

DR. KAY: Neither. Gourmet meals _____ on Earth and then they
4. (will / prepackage)

_____ just _____ on board.
5. (will / warm up)

CM: The space station will have an international crew. In your opinion, how

_____ food _____ to suit everyone's taste?
6. (should / select)

DR. KAY: Foods from all participating countries _____. I think a food
7. (have to / offer)

preference form _____ by each new member. Then, foods
8. (should / fill out)

_____ from the forms.
9. (can / select)

CM: _____ dishes _____ on board?
10. (Will / use)

DR. KAY: Probably. And utensils _____ to the plates so they won't fly
11. (will / attach)

around. Meals _____ as pleasant as possible.
12. (should / make)

CM: I know that sleep is really important too. _____ sleeping quarters

_____ by several crew members?
13. (Will / share)

DR. KAY: We hope not. We've learned from other programs that privacy is very important.

In my opinion, each crew member _____ with private sleeping
14. (must / provide)

quarters. Everyone needs space for personal items.

CM: What else _____ from other space programs?
15. (can / learn)

DR. KAY: Earlier vehicles didn't provide enough windows for viewing the Earth.

CM: _____ more windows _____?
16. (Could / provide)

DR. KAY: Sure. And some windows even _____ in the astronauts' private
17. (ought to / place)

quarters as well.

CM: Thanks, Dr. Kay. You've given us a fascinating picture of life in space.

3 AFTER THE SIMULATION

Some scientists who are going to join the space station have just completed a simulation of life on the station. Complete their conversations, using the modals in parentheses and correct verbs from the boxes.

design	improve	keep	remove	~~solve~~

KENT: These simulations are useful.

LYLE: Yes. They really give you a feeling of what it'll be like to live in space.

KENT: There are still some problems, though. I just hope that they

_____can be solved_____ before the real thing.
1. (can)

GINA: It was uncomfortably warm in there. What was the temperature?

CESÁR: I don't know. But it _____ at 68°.
2. (should)

GINA: For me, that's still warm. The material they use in our clothing

_____ .
3. (ought to)

CESÁR: Or maybe it _____ in layers so that the top layer
4. (could)

_____ if it gets too warm.
5. (can)

conduct	deliver	do	give	store

HANS: I didn't like the food very much.

HISA: Me neither. We _____ more fresh food.
6. (ought to)

HANS: That takes up too much room. But remember, fresh fruit and vegetables

_____ by the shuttle every few weeks.
7. (be going to)

HISA: What _____ with all the trash? Space litter is already a
8. (will)

big problem!

HANS: I'm sure it _____ on board and then removed and brought back
9. (will)

to Earth by the shuttle.

LUIS: When I shaved, the whisker dust kept flying back in my face.

EGOR: Some experiments _____ on the long-term health effects of
10. (should)

inhaling it.

4 EDITING

Read an astronaut's journal notes. Find and correct eight mistakes in the use of the passive with modals and modal-like expressions. The first mistake is already corrected.

Oct. 4

6:15 A.M.

I used the sleeping restraints last night, so my feet and hands didn't float around as much.

I slept a lot better. I'm going to suggest some changes in the restraints though—I think

they ought to be ~~make~~ *made* more comfortable. I felt really trapped. And maybe these sleeping

quarters could designed differently. They're too small.

10:45 A.M.

My face is all puffy, and my eyes are red. Exercise helps a little—I'd better be gotten on

the exercise bike right away. I can be misunderstanding very easily when I look like this.

Sometimes people think I've been crying. And yesterday Max thought I was angry when

he turned on *Star Trek*. Actually, I love that show.

1:00 P.M.

Lunch was pretty good. Chicken Teriyaki. It's nice and spicy, and the sauce can actually

been tasted, even at zero gravity. Some more of it had better be flown in on the Shuttle

pretty soon. It's the most popular dish in the freezer.

4:40 P.M.

I'm worried about Kristen. Just before I left on this mission, she said she was planning to

quit school at the end of the semester. That's only a month away. I want to call her and

discuss it. But I worry that I might get angry and yell. I

might overheard by the others. They really should figure

out some way to give us more privacy.

10:30 P.M.

The view of Earth is unbelievably breathtaking! My

favorite time is spent looking out the window—watching

Earth pass below. At night a halo of light surrounds the

horizon. It's so bright that the tops of the clouds can

see. It can't be described. It simply have to be

experienced.

COMMUNICATION PRACTICE

5 LISTENING

Some crew members aboard the space station are watching television. Listen and read the script below. Then listen again and circle the underlined words you hear.

PICARRO: Spaceship *Endeavor* calling Earth. . . . This is Captain Picarro speaking. We've been hit by a meteorite.

EARTH: Is anyone hurt?

PICARRO: No, everyone is safe.

EARTH: You'd better start repairing the damage immediately.

PICARRO: It <u>can</u> / <u>can't</u> be repaired out here.
1.

★ ★ ★ ★ ★ ★ ★

PICARRO: We'll be approaching Planet CX5 of the Delta solar system in a few hours. Is their language on our computer, Dr. Sock?

SOCK: I'm checking now. . . . We don't have a language for CX5 on the computer, but we have one for CX4. Shall we try it?

PICARRO: We'd better be very careful. Our messages <u>could</u> / <u>should</u> be misunderstood.
2.

★ ★ ★ ★ ★ ★ ★

LON: OK. I'm ready. Let's go.

RAY: What about oxygen?

LON: Isn't the atmosphere on CX5 just like Earth's?

RAY: I think you've been in space too long. Read your manual. Oxygen <u>must</u> / <u>must not</u> be used on all other planets.
3.

★ ★ ★ ★ ★ ★ ★

PICARRO: I've lost contact with Lon and Ray. I hope their equipment works on CX5.

SOCK: Don't worry. <u>They'll pick up the radar</u> / <u>They'll be picked up by the radar</u>.
4.

★ ★ ★ ★ ★ ★ ★

LON: Look at those plants. I want to take some back to the ship.

RAY: They <u>can</u> / <u>can't</u> be grown in space. We've already tried.
5.

LON: That's right. I forgot.

★ ★ ★ ★ ★ ★ ★

CX5 LEADER: What do you want to ask us, Earthlings?

RAY: Our vehicle was hit by a meteorite. We request permission to land on your planet.

CX5 LEADER: Permission granted. Our engineers will be ready for you.

RAY: Thank you. As you know, we <u>have to help</u> / <u>have to be helped</u> with the repairs.
6.

6 CLOSE QUARTERS

Work in small groups. Imagine that in preparation for a space mission, you and your classmates are going to spend a week together in a one-room apartment. You will not be able to leave the apartment for the entire time. Make a list of rules for yourselves. Use the passive with modals and modal-like expressions. Compare your list with that of another group.

Some Issues to Consider:

Food

Clothes

Room temperature

Noise

Neatness

Cleanliness

Privacy

Language

Entertainment

Other: _____

EXAMPLE:
Dinner will be served at 6:00 P.M.
The dishes must be washed after each meal.

7 MONEY FOR SPACE

Sending people to the space station costs about $16,000 an hour. Should money be spent for these space projects, or could it be spent better on Earth? If so, how? Discuss these questions with your classmates.

EXAMPLE:
A: I think space projects are useful. A lot of new products are going to be developed in space.
B: I don't agree. Some of that money should be spent on public housing.

8 WHAT SHOULD BE DONE?

Work in small groups. Look at the picture of a student lounge. You are responsible for getting it in order, but you have limited time and money. Agree on five things that should be done.

EXAMPLE:
A: The window has to be replaced.
B: No. That'll cost too much. It can just be taped.
C: That'll look terrible. It should be replaced.
D: OK. What else should be done?

9 WRITING

Write two paragraphs about your neighborhood, your school, or your place of work. In your first paragraph write about what might be done to improve it. In your second paragraph, write about what shouldn't be changed.

EXAMPLE:
I enjoy attending this school, but I believe some things could be improved.
First, I think that more software should be purchased for the language lab. . . .

20 THE PASSIVE CAUSATIVE

GRAMMAR **IN CONTEXT**

BEFORE YOU READ Look at the pictures. Which forms of body art do you think are attractive?

Read this article from a fashion magazine.

Body Art

Each culture has a different ideal of beauty, and throughout the ages, men and women have done amazing things to achieve the ideal. They have **had** *their hair* **shaved, cut, colored, straightened,** and **curled**; and they have **had** *their bodies* **decorated** with painting and tattoos. Here are some of today's many options.

HAIR. Getting *your hair* done is the easiest way to change your appearance. Today, both men and women **have** *their hair* **permed**. This chemical procedure can curl hair or just give it more body. If your hair is long, you can, of course, **get** *it* **cut**, but did you know that you can also **have** *short hair* **lengthened**? You **can have** *hair extensions* **added** to your own hair, and the effect can be either conservative or very far out. You can **have** *your hair* **colored** and become a blonde, brunette, or

redhead, but you can also **have** *it* **bleached** white or **get** *it* **dyed** blue, green, or orange. (You can wash out the wilder colors.)

(continued on next page)

Body Art (continued)

TATTOOS. This form of body art was created thousands of years ago. Today, tattoos have again become popular. More and more people—both in offices and on college campuses—are **having** *them* **done**. However, caution is necessary. Tattoo needles can spread disease, so the tattoo artist must be well-trained in preventing infection. Although you can now **get** *a tattoo* **removed** with less pain and scarring than before, **having** *one* **applied** is still a big decision.

BODY PAINT. If a tattoo is not for you, you can **have** *ornaments* **painted** on your skin instead. Some people **have** *necklaces and bracelets* **painted** on their neck and arms or **get** *a butterfly mask* **applied** to their face for a special party. Unlike a tattoo, these decorations can be washed off.

PIERCING. Pierced ears are an old favorite, but lately the practice of piercing has expanded. Many people now **get** *several holes* **pierced** in each ear. **Getting** *the nose, lip, or other parts of the body* **pierced** for jewelry is also more common. **Having** *piercing* **performed** requires even more caution than tattooing, and after care is very important.

COSMETIC SURGERY. You can **get** *your nose* **shortened**, or **have** *your chin* **lengthened**. If wrinkles make you look like you're always frowning, you can **get** *them* **filled in** with a collagen injection (it only lasts four months, and costs about $350). You can even **have** *the shape of your body* **changed** with liposuction, a process that removes fat cells. There is some risk involved, so the decision to have cosmetic surgery requires thought.

Some ways of changing your appearance may be cheap and temporary. However, others are expensive and permanent. So, think before you act, and don't let today's choice become tomorrow's regret.

—By Debra Santana

GRAMMAR **PRESENTATION**
THE PASSIVE CAUSATIVE

STATEMENTS

SUBJECT	*HAVE / GET*	OBJECT	PAST PARTICIPLE	(*BY* + AGENT)	
She	**has**	*her hair*	**cut**	*by André*	every month.
He	**has had**	*his beard*	**trimmed**		before.
I	**get**	*my nails*	**done**		at André's.
She	**is going to get**	*her ears*	**pierced.**		

YES / NO QUESTIONS

AUXILIARY VERB	SUBJECT	*HAVE / GET*	OBJECT	PAST PARTICIPLE	(*BY* + AGENT)
Does	she	**have**	*her hair*	**cut**	*by André?*
Has	he	**had**	*his beard*	**trimmed?**	
Do	you	**get**	*your nails*	**done?**	
Is	she	**going to get**	*her ears*	**pierced?**	

WH- QUESTIONS

WH- WORD	AUXILIARY VERB	SUBJECT	*HAVE / GET*	OBJECT	PAST PARTICIPLE	(*BY* + AGENT)
How often	**does**	she	**have**	*her hair*	**cut**	*by André?*
Where	**did**	he	**get**	*his beard*	**trimmed?**	
When	**do**	you	**get**	*your nails*	**done?**	
Why	**is**	she	**going to get**	*her ears*	**pierced?**	

NOTES	**EXAMPLES**
1. Form the **passive causative** with the appropriate form of *have* or *get* + object + past participle. The passive causative can be used in <u>all tenses</u> and with <u>modals</u>.	• I always **have *my hair*** cut by André. • I **haven't had *it*** done since June. • Last year I **got *my coat*** cleaned once. • Next week I**'m going to have *my windows*** washed. • I**'m getting *them*** done by Spotless. • I **had *them*** washed a long time ago. • You **should get *the car*** checked. • You **ought to have *it*** done soon.
2. Use the passive causative to talk about <u>services that you arrange for someone to do for you</u>. ▶ **BE CAREFUL!** Do not confuse the simple past causative with the past perfect.	• I used to color my own hair, but now I **have *it*** colored. • André is going to **get *his hair salon* remodeled** by a local architect. **SIMPLE PAST CAUSATIVE** • I **had *it*** done last week. *(Someone did it for me.)* **PAST PERFECT** • I **had done** it before. *(I did it myself.)*
3. Use *by* when it is necessary to mention the <u>person doing the service</u> (the agent). (*See Unit 18, page 273 for information on when to include the agent.*)	• Where does Lynne **get her hair done**? NOT Where does Lynne get her hair done ~~by a hair stylist~~? **BUT:** • This time she**'s getting her hair done *by a new stylist*.**
4. BE CAREFUL! Do not confuse the expression *to get something done* (*to finish something*) with the passive causative. The context will usually make the meaning clear.	• I had a lot of homework. But I worked hard and **got it done** before 11 P.M. *(I finished my homework before 11 P.M.)* **A:** Your hair looks good. **B:** I **got it done** at André's. *(André did my hair for me.)*

FOCUSED PRACTICE

1 DISCOVER THE GRAMMAR

Read the conversations. Then decide if the statements are **True (T)** *or* **False (F)**.

1. **JAKE:** Have you finished writing your new article?

   DEBRA: Yes. I'm going to get it copied and then take it to the post office.

   ___F___ Debra is going to copy the article herself.

2. **DEBRA:** I'm glad that's done. Now I can start planning for our party.

   JAKE: Me too. I'm going to get my hair cut tomorrow after work.

   _____ Jake cuts his own hair.

3. **DEBRA:** Speaking about hair—Amber, *your* hair's getting awfully long.

   AMBER: I know, Mom. I'm cutting it tomorrow.

   _____ Amber cuts her own hair.

4. **AMBER:** Mom, why didn't you get your nails done last time you went to the hairdresser?

   DEBRA: Because I had done them just before my appointment.

   _____ Debra did her own nails.

5. **AMBER:** I was thinking of painting a butterfly on my forehead for the party.

   DEBRA: A butterfly! Well, OK. As long as it washes off.

   _____ Someone is going to paint a butterfly on Amber's forehead for her.

6. **DEBRA:** Jake, do you think we should get the floors waxed before the party?

   JAKE: I think they look OK. We'll get them done afterward.

   _____ Debra and Jake are going to hire someone to wax their floors after the party.

7. **DEBRA:** I'm going to watch some TV and then go to bed. What's on the agenda for tomorrow?

   JAKE: I have to get up early. I'm getting the car washed before work.

   _____ Jake is going to wash the car himself.

8. **DEBRA:** You know, I think it's time to change the oil, too.

   JAKE: You're right. I'll do it this weekend.

   _____ Jake is going to change the oil himself.

2 ESSENTIAL SERVICES

It's February 15. Look at the Santanas' calendar and write sentences about when they had things done, and when they are going to have things done.

February

Sunday	Monday	Tuesday	Wednesday	Thursday	Friday	Saturday
1	2	3	4	5	6	7 Deb— hairdresser
8	9	10	11	12 Jake— barber	13 carpets	14 dog groomer
15 TODAY'S DATE	16 windows	17	18	19	20 food and drinks	21 party!!
22	23	24	25 Amber— ears pierced	26	27	28 family pictures

1. The Santanas / have / family pictures / take

   The Santanas are going to have family pictures taken on the 28th.

2. Debra / get / her hair / perm

   _____

3. Amber / have / the dog / groom

   _____

4. They / get / the windows / wash

   _____

5. They / have / the carpets / clean

   _____

6. Amber / have / her ears / pierce

   _____

7. Jake / get / his hair / cut

   _____

8. They / have / food and drinks / deliver

   _____

❸ GETTING THINGS DONE

Debra and Jake are going to have a party. Complete the conversations with the passive causative of the appropriate verbs in the box.

| color | cut | develop | dry clean | paint | repair | ~~shorten~~ | wash |

1. **AMBER:** I bought a new dress for the party, Mom. What do you think of it?

   DEBRA: It's pretty, but it's a little long. Why don't you _____ get it shortened _____?

   AMBER: OK. They do alterations at the cleaners. I'll take it in tomorrow.

2. **AMBER:** By the way, what are *you* planning to wear?

   DEBRA: My blue silk dress. I'm glad you reminded me. I'd better _____.

   AMBER: I can drop it off at the cleaners with my dress.

3. **JAKE:** The house is ready, except for the windows. They look pretty dirty.

   DEBRA: Don't worry. We _____ tomorrow.

4. **DEBRA:** Amber, your hair is getting really long. I thought you were going to cut it.

   AMBER: I decided not to do it myself this time. I _____ by André.

5. **DEBRA:** My hair's getting a lot of gray in it. Should I _____?

   JAKE: It looks fine to me, but it's up to you.

6. **AMBER:** Mom, someone's at the door and it's only twelve o'clock!

   DEBRA: No, it's not. The clock stopped again.

   JAKE: I don't believe it! I _____ already _____ twice this year, and it's only February!

7. **GUEST:** The house looks beautiful, Jake. _____ you _____?

   JAKE: No, actually we did it ourselves last summer.

8. **DEBRA:** I have one shot left in the camera. Come on, everyone! Say "cheese"!

   GUESTS: Cheese!

   DEBRA: Great. We took three rolls of pictures today. Maybe we can

   _____ before Mom and Dad go back to Florida.

COMMUNICATION PRACTICE

4 LISTENING

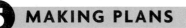 *Amber has just gone to college. Listen to her conversation with Jake. Then listen again and check the correct column.*

	Amber did the job herself	Amber hired someone to do the job
1. Change the oil in her car.	☐	☑
2. Change the locks.	☐	☐
3. Paint the apartment.	☐	☐
4. Put up bookshelves.	☐	☐
5. Bring new furniture to the apartment.	☐	☐
6. Paint her hands.	☐	☐
7. Cut her hair.	☐	☐
8. Color her hair.	☐	☐

5 MAKING PLANS

Work in groups. Imagine that you are taking a car trip together to another country. You'll be gone for several weeks. Decide where you're going. Then make a list of things you have to do and arrange before the trip. Use the ideas below and your own.

Passport and visas

Car (oil, gas, tires, seatbelts)

Home (pets, plants, mail, newspaper delivery)

Personal (clothing, hair)

Medical (teeth, eyes, prescriptions for medicine)

Other: _____

> **EXAMPLE:**
> **A:** I have to get my passport renewed.
> **B:** Me, too. And we should apply for visas right away.

Now compare your list with that of another group. Did you forget anything?

⑥ TOTAL MAKEOVER

*Work with a partner. Look at the **Before** and **After** pictures of a fashion model. You have five minutes to find and write down all the things the model had done to change her appearance.*

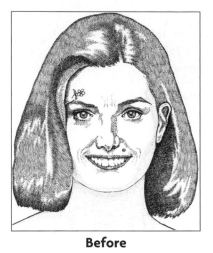

Before

After

EXAMPLE:
She had her nose shortened.

When the five minutes are up, compare your list with that of another pair. Then look at the pictures again to check your answers.

⑦ WHAT DO YOU THINK?

*Work with a partner. Look at the **Before** and **After** pictures in Exercise 6. Do you think the model looks better? Why or why not?*

EXAMPLE:
A: I don't know why she had her nose fixed.
B: Neither do I. I think it looked fine before.

⑧ BEAUTY TALK

Work in small groups. Think about other cultures. Discuss the types of things people get done in order to change their appearance. Report back to your class.

EXAMPLE:
In India women get their hands painted for special occasions.
I think it looks very nice.

⑨ WRITING

Write a short letter to someone you know. Tell about your activities. Include things that you have recently done or have had done. Also talk about things you are going to do or are going to have done.

REVIEW OR SELFTEST

I. *Circle the active or passive form of the verbs to complete the conversation with a travel agent.*

LINDSAY: This is Lindsay Boyle from AL Metals. I

(didn't receive)/ wasn't received my airline tickets today, and
1.

I leave / 'm left for Jamaica in two days.
2.

AGENT: Let me check. Hmmm. That's strange. The tickets

mailed / were mailed a week ago. You should be had / have them
3.   4.

by now.

LINDSAY: How about my hotel reservations?

AGENT: Those made / were made for you last week. They
5.

confirmed / were confirmed by the Hotel Mariel today. Will you
6.

need / be needed a car when you arrive?
7.

LINDSAY: Not right away. I'll be met / meet at the airport by my client. I'll
8.

probably rent / be rented a car later on. Oh, the receptionist
9.

was just handed / just handed me a note. The tickets are here. They
10.

were sent / sent to the wrong floor.
11.

AGENT: Sorry about that.

LINDSAY: Never mind. We have them now, so no harm did / was done.
12.

II. *Complete the conversations with the modal and the passive form of the verbs in parentheses.*

LINDSAY: _____Will_____ the reports _____be printed_____ by the end of
                                          1. (Will / print)

next week?

TED: Sure. In fact they _____ to the office by Tuesday.
                              2. (might / deliver)

LINDSAY: Good. I hope they turn out well. They _____ by a lot
                                                  3. (will / read)

of people.

(continued on next page)

Ted: Don't worry. This company always does nice work. I'm sure you

_____ when you see them.
4. (will / satisfy)

Lindsay: Oh, by the way, those reports _____ for shipment as soon as they
5. (have to / pack)

arrive. I'm taking them with me to Jamaica.

Ted: I didn't know you planned to bring them. I _____ things like that.
6. (ought to / tell)

So how long are you staying?

Lindsay: About a week. But my stay _____. It depends on how things go.
7. (could / extend)

Ted: You know, your office _____ while you're gone. And your computer
8. (should / paint)

_____. So maybe you should stay another week.
9. (have to / service)

Lindsay: I think that _____. I hear it's a pretty nice place.
10. (can / arrange)

III. *Circle the letter of the correct words to complete these sentences.*

1. Reggae music is _____ at Jamaica's Sunsplash Festival. A B Ⓒ D
(A) perform (C) performed
(B) performing (D) performs

2. This wonderful festival _____ be missed. A B C D
(A) isn't (C) shouldn't
(B) wasn't (D) hasn't

3. Music lovers from all over the world can _____ found at the A B C D
festival.
(A) be (C) been
(B) have (D) were

4. Swimmers and divers _____ Jamaica's beautiful beaches. A B C D
(A) are enjoyed (C) enjoys
(B) enjoy (D) are enjoyed by

5. Go deep-sea fishing, and get your picture _____ with
your catch. A B C D
(A) taken (C) took
(B) taking (D) be taken

6. Jamaica _____ avoided in the fall because of dangerous A B C D
storms.
(A) ought to (C) should have
(B) should (D) ought to be

7. Jamaica was settled _____ people from Africa and Europe.   **A B C D**
    (A) at   (C) from
    (B) by   (D) of

8. In the early days, many languages could _____ in Jamaica.   **A B C D**
    (A) be heard   (C) heard
    (B) were heard   (D) hear

9. Today Creole, a mixture of languages, _____ spoken widely.   **A B C D**
    (A) was   (C) is
    (B) were   (D) are

10. Tickets _____ from any travel agent or directly from the airline.   **A B C D**
    (A) may be purchased   (C) purchase
    (B) may purchase   (D) purchased

11. The last time, I _____ my ticket sent directly to my office.   **A B C D**
    (A) have   (C) was
    (B) get   (D) had

IV. *Complete the memo with* **have** *or* **get** *and the correct form of the verb in parentheses.*

I'd like to _____have_____ some work _____done_____ in my office, and this
                                           1. (do)

seems like a good time for it. Please _____ my carpet _____
                                               2. (clean)

while I'm gone. And while you're at it, could you _____ my computer and

printer _____? It's been quite a while since they've been serviced. Ted wants
             3. (look at)

to _____ my office _____ while I'm gone. Please tell him any
                          4. (paint)

color is fine except pink.

Last week, I _____ some new brochures _____. Please call the
                                     5. (design)

printer and _____ them _____ directly to the sales reps. And could
                             6. (deliver)

you _____ more business cards _____ too? We're almost out.
                                   7. (make up)

When I get back, it will be time to plan the holiday party. I think we _____

it _____ this year. While I'm gone, why don't you call around and get some
   8. (cater)

estimates from caterers? _____ the estimates _____ to Ted.
                                       9. (send)

               See you in two weeks!

               Lindsay

V. *Complete these facts about Jamaica with a passive form of the verbs in the box. Include the agent in parentheses only where necessary.*

~~discover~~   employ   export   grow   listen to   popularize   strike

1. Jamaica ___was discovered by Europeans___ on May 4, 1494, during Columbus's
                        (Europeans)
   second voyage.

2. Some of the best coffee in the world _____ on the slopes
                                              (coffee growers)
   of Jamaica's Blue Mountains.

3. About 50,000 people _____.
                          (the sugar industry)

4. Sugar _____ to many countries.
            (sugar producers)

5. The island _____ about once every eight years, but few
                     (hurricanes)
   have caused severe damage.

6. Reggae music originated in Jamaica. It _____ in the 1970s.
                                                (Bob Marley)

7. Now it _____ everywhere.
             (people)

VI. *Each sentence has four underlined words or phrases. The four underlined parts of the sentences are marked A, B, C, or D. Circle the letter of the <u>one</u> underlined word or phrase that is NOT CORRECT.*

1. The reports <u>were</u> <u>arrived</u> late, so I <u>had</u> <u>them sent</u> to you this morning.   Ⓐ B C D
           A   B   C   D

2. Some mistakes <u>were</u> <u>made</u> in the brochure, but they might <u>corrected</u>   A B C D
               A   B   C
   before you <u>get</u> back.
            D

3. You<u>'ll see</u> a copy before they<u>'re</u> <u>printed</u> <u>by the printer</u>.   A B C D
       A   B   C   D

4. A funny thing <u>was</u> happened when your <u>office</u> <u>was</u> <u>painted</u> yesterday.   A B C D
                A   B   C   D

5. Your office almost <u>got</u> <u>painted</u> pink, but we <u>had</u> the painters <u>used</u>   A B C D
                  A   B   C   D
   white instead.

6. An estimate from the party caterer <u>were</u> <u>left</u> on my desk, but we've   A B C D
                                    A   B
   <u>got</u> <u>to wait</u> for your decision.
    C   D

7. <u>Has</u> your stay <u>been</u> <u>extended</u>, or will you <u>be returned</u> next week?   A B C D
     A   B   C   D

▶ *To check your answers, go to the Answer Key on page 311.*

From Grammar to Writing Changing the Focus with Passive Verbs

When you write a report, you often want to focus on the results of an action rather than the people who performed the action. Use the passive to focus on the results.

EXAMPLE:
Artists **carved** many wooden statues for the temple. ⟶
Many wooden statues **were carved** for the temple.

1 *Read the following report about a famous building in Korea. Underline the passive forms.*

Two Buddhist monks built Haeinsa Temple in 802 A.D. The king gave them the money to build the temple after the two monks saved his queen's life. Haeinsa burned down in 1817, but <u>the Main Hall was rebuilt</u> in 1818 on its original foundations.

Today, Haeinsa is composed of several large, beautiful buildings. It contains many paintings and statues. Someone carved three of the statues from a single ancient tree. Behind the Main Hall is a steep flight of stone stairs that lead to the Storage Buildings. These buildings, which escaped the fire, were constructed in 1488 in order to store wooden printing blocks of Buddhist texts. It was believed that these printing blocks could protect the country against invaders. Monks carved the 81,258 wooden blocks in the 13th century. A century later, nuns carried them to Haeinsa for safekeeping. Architects designed the Storage Buildings to preserve the wooden blocks. For more than five hundred years, the blocks have been kept in perfect condition because of the design of these buildings. Haeinsa, which means *reflection on a smooth sea*, is also known as the Temple of Teaching because it houses the ancient printing blocks.

2 *Find five sentences that would be better expressed in the passive. Rewrite them.*

a. Haeinsa Temple was built by two Buddhist monks in 802 A.D.

b. _____

c. _____

d. _____

e. _____

3 *Answer these questions about Haeinsa Temple.*

a. When was it built? _802 A.D._____

b. Who built it? _____

c. Why was it built? _____

d. What are some of its features? _____

e. What is it famous for? _____

4 *Before you write . . .*

• Choose a famous building to write about. Get information from a book or the Internet. Answer the questions in Exercise 3.

• Work with a partner. Ask and answer questions about your topic.

5 *Write a report about the building you researched. Use the passive where appropriate. If possible, include a photograph or drawing of the building.*

6 *Exchange paragraphs with a different partner. Answer the questions below.*

a. Did the writer answer all the questions in Exercise 3? _____

b. What interested you the most about the building? _____

c. What would you like to know more about? _____

d. Did the writer use the passive appropriately? _____

e. Are the past participles correct? _____

REVIEW OR SELFTEST
ANSWER KEY

I. (Units 18–19)
2. leave
3. were mailed
4. have
5. were made
6. were confirmed
7. need
8. be met
9. rent
10. just handed
11. were sent
12. was done

II. (Unit 19)
2. might be delivered
3. 'll be read
4. 'll be satisfied
5. have to be packed
6. ought to be told
7. could be extended
8. should be painted
9. has to be serviced
10. can be arranged

III. (Units 18–20)
2. C   7. B
3. A   8. A
4. B   9. C
5. A   10. A
6. D   11. D

IV. (Unit 20)
2. have OR get . . . cleaned
3. have OR get . . . looked at
4. have OR get . . . painted
5. had OR got . . . designed
6. have OR get . . . delivered
7. have OR get . . . made up
8. 'll have OR 'll get . . . catered
9. Have OR Get . . . sent

V. (Units 18–20)
2. is grown
3. are employed by the sugar industry
4. is exported
5. is struck by hurricanes
6. was popularized by Bob Marley
7. 's listened to

VI. (Units 18–20)
2. C   5. D
3. D   6. A
4. A   7. D

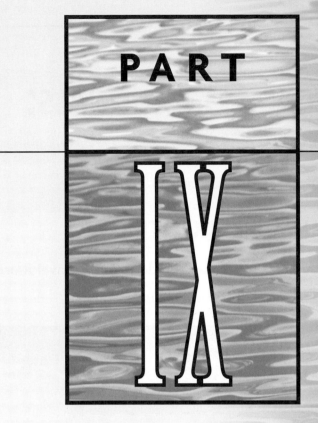

PART

IX

CONDITIONALS

21

FACTUAL CONDITIONALS: PRESENT

GRAMMAR **IN CONTEXT**

BEFORE YOU READ   What do you do to make travel more comfortable?

Read the brochure about airline travel.

Know Before You Go

High-speed air travel is usually fast and efficient. However, it has its special hassles, and these can cause delay and discomfort if you don't know how to avoid them. Know before you go, and enjoy your journey more.

RECONFIRMING. If you are traveling internationally, you should reconfirm your flight 72 hours ahead of time. In spite of electronic reservation systems, many airlines rely on your telephone call to reserve your seat.

CHECKING IN. A good travel agent can often get you a boarding pass in advance. However, even with a previously issued boarding pass, you should still check in at the gate. **You could be bumped from a flight if you don't.**

MEALS. If you need a low-calorie, low-sodium, or low-cholesterol meal, order it in advance from the airline. You can also order vegetarian and kosher meals ahead of time. **If you hate airplane food** (and many people do), **then you might order one of these special meals anyway.** It will be fresher and taste better than the standard meal. And you will be served before anyone else.

Know Before You Go

COMFORT. One common case of discomfort on a plane is dehydration. To avoid this problem, drink a glass of juice or water every hour you are on the plane.

Sitting in one place for too long is another cause. **If you move around the cabin every hour, you can avoid stiffness.**

JET LAG. There's no way to avoid it. **If you travel across time zones at high**

speeds, your internal clock doesn't keep up with the time changes. That's why your body thinks it's midnight when it's really 9:00 A.M. To minimize the discomfort, reset your watch for the time zone of your destination before you leave. Also, arrange to arrive late in the day. **You are psychologically prepared to sleep at the right time if it's evening when you get to your destination.**

WHEELCHAIR FLYERS. Airline wheelchairs are heavy, and someone must push you from behind. **You have much more mobility if you store your own wheelchair in the cabin.** Terry Winkler, a physician who is paraplegic, gives this advice: **"If my wheelchair can't be stored on board, I insist that they bring it from the baggage compartment as soon as the plane lands."** If you have a disability, be aware of your rights as a passenger.

FLYING WITH CHILDREN. If you are traveling with children, your big challenge is to stay together on the plane. Ask for seats as early as possible (thirty days before your flight). **If you get scattered seats, preboard and ask the flight attendant to help you.** He or she may be able to reassemble your family before the flight.

GRAMMAR **PRESENTATION**
FACTUAL CONDITIONALS: PRESENT

STATEMENTS	
IF CLAUSE	**RESULT CLAUSE**
If it **snows,**	the airport **closes.**
it**'s** very cold,	planes **can't leave.**

STATEMENTS		
RESULT CLAUSE	**IF CLAUSE**	
The airport **closes**	if	it **snows.**
Planes **can't leave**		it**'s** very cold.

YES / NO QUESTIONS		
RESULT CLAUSE	**IF CLAUSE**	
Does the airport **close**	if	it **snows?**
Can planes **leave**		it**'s** cold?

SHORT ANSWERS	
AFFIRMATIVE	
Yes,	it **does.**
	they **can.**

SHORT ANSWERS	
NEGATIVE	
No,	it **doesn't.**
	they **can't.**

WH- QUESTIONS	
RESULT CLAUSE	**IF CLAUSE**
Why **does** air **get** lighter	**if** it **expands?**

NOTES

EXAMPLES

1. Use **present factual conditional** sentences to talk about <u>general truths</u> and <u>scientific facts</u>.

The *if* clause talks about the condition, and the result clause talks about what happens if the condition occurs.

Use the <u>simple present tense</u> in both clauses.

     if clause   result clause
- ***If*** it**'s** noon in Lima, it**'s** 6:00 P.M. in Rome.

     if clause   result clause
- ***If*** air **expands**, it **becomes** lighter.

2. You can also use **factual conditional** sentences to talk about <u>habits</u> and <u>recurring events</u> (things that happen again and again).

Use the <u>simple present tense or present progressive</u> in the *if* clause. Use the <u>simple present tense</u> in the result clause.

     if clause   result clause
- ***If*** Bill **flies**, he **orders** a special meal.

     if clause   result clause
- ***If*** I**'m traveling** far, I always **fly**.

3. You can use **modals** in the result clause.	• If you practice your Chinese, you *can improve* quickly. • If you shop in open-air markets, you *shouldn't* **wear** expensive clothes. • If you wear expensive clothes, shopkeepers *might* **charge** you more.
4. Use the **imperative** in the result clause to give <u>instructions, commands</u>, and <u>invitations</u> that depend on a certain condition. USAGE NOTE: We sometimes use *then* to <u>emphasize the result</u> in factual conditional sentences with imperatives or modals.	• If you like it hot, **travel** in July. • If the seat belt light is on, **don't leave** your seat. • If you come to Tokyo, **stay** with us. • If you like it hot, *then* **travel** in July. • If you shop in open-air markets, *then* you **shouldn't wear** expensive clothes.
5. You can begin conditional sentences with the *if* clause or the result clause. The meaning is the same. ▶ **BE CAREFUL!** Use a comma between the two clauses only when the *if* clause comes first.	• **If the seat belt light goes on,** buckle your seat belt. OR • Buckle your seat belt **if the seat belt light goes on**.
6. You can make either or both clauses <u>negative</u> in conditional sentences.	• If I'm traveling far, I fly. • If I'm **not** traveling far, I drive. • If I'm traveling far, I **don't** drive. • If I'm **not** traveling far, I **don't** fly.
7. You can often use *when* or *whenever* instead of *if*. This is especially true when you talk about <u>general truths</u>, <u>habits</u>, and <u>recurring events</u>.	• *When* it's noon in Lima, it's 6:00 P.M. in Rome. • *When(ever)* Bill flies, he orders a special meal. • *When(ever)* the flight is bumpy, I keep my seat belt buckled.

FOCUSED PRACTICE

1 DISCOVER THE GRAMMAR

In each factual conditional sentence, underline the result clause once. Underline the clause that expresses the condition twice.

<u><u>If you run into problems on your journey</u></u>, <u>know your rights as a passenger</u>. Often the airline company is required to compensate you for delays or damages. For example, the airline provides meals and hotel rooms if a flight is unduly delayed. However, the airline owes you a lot more if it caused the delay by overbooking. This occurs mostly during holidays, when airlines often sell more tickets than there are seats. If all the passengers actually show up, then the flight is overbooked. Airlines usually award upgrades or additional free travel to passengers who volunteer to take a later flight. However, if no one volunteers, your flight may be delayed. In that case, the airline must repay you 100 percent of the cost of your ticket for a delay of up to four hours on an international flight. Whenever the delay is more than four hours, you receive 200 percent of the cost of your ticket.

Suppose you arrive on time, but your suitcase doesn't. Ask for funds to buy clothing or toiletries if your luggage doesn't get there when you do. The airline should award you $25 to $50. If the airline actually loses your suitcase, then it must pay you the value of its contents. The limit is $1,250 for a domestic flight and $9 a pound for an international flight.

2 IF YOU'RE IN HONG KONG   Grammar Notes 1–4

Read these conversations about Hong Kong. Summarize the advice with conditional sentences.

1. **A:** I hate hot weather.

   B: The best time to go to Hong Kong is November or December.

   > If you hate hot weather, the best time to
   > go to Hong Kong is November or December.

   The weather is cooler then.

2. A: I'm traveling with my children.

B: Take them to Lai Chi Kok Amusement Park in Kowloon.

_____

They'll enjoy the games, shows, and rides.

3. A: We need a moderate-priced hotel.

B: I suggest Harbour View International House.

_____

It's a good hotel, and it's fairly inexpensive.

4. A: We like seafood.

B: There are wonderful seafood restaurants on Lamma Island.

_____

You can take the Star Ferry there.

5. A: I'm fascinated by Chinese opera.

B: You might like the street opera in the Shanghai Street Night Market.

_____

Opera is also performed at City Hall.

6. A: I'd like to get a good view of Hong Kong.

B: You should take the funicular to the Peak.

_____

There's a great view of the harbor from there.

7. A: I'm interested in buying some traditional Chinese crafts.

B: Then you ought to visit the Western District on Hong Kong Island.

_____

You can buy things like fans and mahjong tiles there.

8. A: I'm looking for a good dim sum restaurant.

B: Try Luk Yu Teahouse on Stanley Street.

_____

It's a historical monument as well as a restaurant.

3 FREQUENT FLYER

*Complete the interview with a Skyways flight attendant. Combine the two sentences in parentheses to make a factual conditional sentence. Keep the same order and decide which clause begins with **if**. Make necessary changes in capitalization and punctuation.*

INTERVIEWER: How long are you usually away?

ATTENDANT: If I go to the Bahamas, I have a two-day layover.
1. (I go to the Bahamas. I have a two-day layover.)

INTERVIEWER: What do you do for two days?

ATTENDANT: I spend a lot of time at the pool if I stay at a hotel.
2. (I spend a lot of time at the pool. I stay at a hotel.)

3. (I stay with friends. I spend time with them.)

INTERVIEWER: Sounds nice.

ATTENDANT: _____
4. (It's not so nice. I get a Dracula.)

INTERVIEWER: A Dracula?

ATTENDANT: That's when you fly to Pittsburgh at midnight, spend four hours in the airport, and then fly back to New York.

INTERVIEWER: Who walks the dog and waters the plants when you're away?

ATTENDANT: I share an apartment with three other flight attendants.

5. (You have three roommates. You don't have trouble finding dogwalkers.)

INTERVIEWER: Sounds like a tough job. Is it worth it?

ATTENDANT: Sure.

6. (It's very rewarding. You don't mind hard work.)

INTERVIEWER: What do you like most about it?

ATTENDANT: The travel. I can write my own ticket for any destination on a Skyways route.

7. (A flight has an empty seat. I ride for free.)

INTERVIEWER: Where have you been so far this year?

ATTENDANT: Tokyo, Honolulu, Hong Kong. It's great—except when you can't get back.

INTERVIEWER: What do you mean?

ATTENDANT: _____
8. (A flight is completely booked. You can't get on it.)

INTERVIEWER: Has that ever happened to you?

ATTENDANT: Sure. I've been stranded in some of the most beautiful cities in the world.

④ WHEN IT'S NOON IN MONTREAL . . .   Grammar Note 7

Look at the chart. Write sentences about the cities with clocks. Use the prompts and **when***. Note: the light clocks show daylight hours; the shaded clocks show evening or nighttime.*

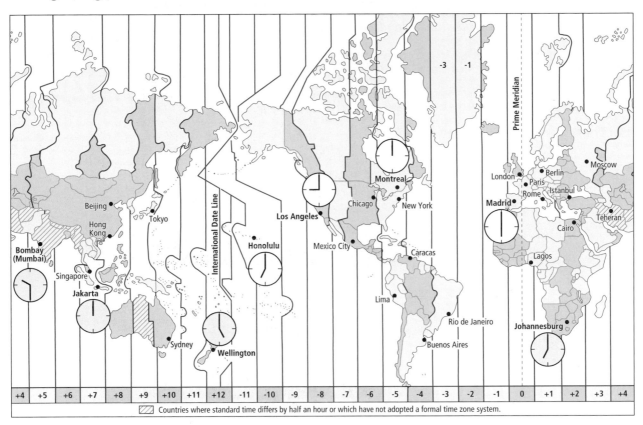

Countries where standard time differs by half an hour or which have not adopted a formal time zone system.

1. When it's noon in Montreal, it's midnight in Jakarta.
   be noon / be midnight

2. When they're watching the sun rise in Honolulu, they're watching the sun set in Johannesburg.
   watch the sun rise / watch the sun set

3. _____
   be midnight / be 6:00 P.M.

4. _____
   eat lunch / eat dinner

5. _____
   get up / go to bed

6. _____
   be 7:00 A.M. / be 7:00 P.M.

7. _____
   begin work / stop work

8. _____
   be 5:00 A.M. / be 9:00 A.M.

COMMUNICATION PRACTICE

5 LISTENING

You and your nephew, Pietro, are flying to Hong Kong by way of Los Angeles. Listen to the announcements. Then read each situation. Listen to the announcements again and check the appropriate box.

	True	False
1. You have two pieces of carry-on luggage and Pietro has one. You can take them on the plane.	☑	☐

2. These are your boarding passes:

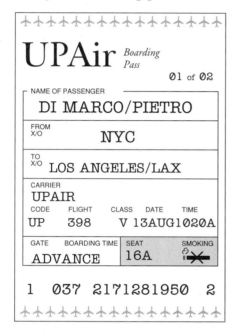

	True	False
You can board now.	☐	☐
3. Look at your boarding passes again. You can board now.	☐	☐
4. Pietro is a child. You should put on his oxygen mask first.	☐	☐
5. You're sitting in a left window seat. You can see the Great Salt Lake.	☐	☐
6. You need information about your connecting flight. You can get this information on the plane.	☐	☐

6 TRAVELING IN COMFORT

Work in small groups. Discuss what you do to stay comfortable when you travel.
Talk about traveling by car, bus, train, and plane.

EXAMPLE:

A: When I travel by car, I stop every three hours.

B: When I travel by car, I always dress comfortably.

7 INFORMATION GAP: IF YOU GO . . .

Work in pairs (A and B). Student B, turn to page 325 and follow the instructions
there. Student A, look at the chart below. Ask your partner questions to complete
the chart. Answer your partner's questions.

	Best Time to Go	Currency	Time: When it's noon in New York . . .
Caracas, Venezuela	December–April	bolívar	1:00 pm.
Istanbul, Turkey	April – October.	Turkesh Lira	8:00 P.M.
Rio de Janeiro, Brazil	April–October	real	2:00 P.M.
Seoul, South Korea	October – March	won	2:00 A.M.*
Vancouver, Canada	July–September	Canadian Dollar	9:00 A.M.
Moscow, Russia	May–September.	ruble	8:00 pm

*the next day

EXAMPLE:

A: If you travel to Caracas, what's the best time to go?

B: December through April.
    What kind of currency do you need if you go there?

A: The bolívar.
    When it's noon in New York, what time is it in Caracas?

When you are done, compare charts. Are they the same?

 **8 TRAVEL TIPS**

Work in small groups. Give and ask for travel advice.

> **EXAMPLE:**
> **A:** If I visit your country, what should I see?
> **B:** If you go to Ecuador you should take a trip to the Galápagos Islands.

9 WHAT HAPPENS IF . . .

Write your typical daily schedule. Exchange schedules with a partner. Ask each other what you do if there are special situations.

> **EXAMPLES:**
> How do you get to work if the bus is late?
> Where do you go if your class is canceled and you have some extra time?

 **10 QUOTABLE QUOTES**

Read these proverbs and quotations about traveling. Discuss them with a partner. Use factual conditional sentences to explain what each one means.

If you travel by boat, prepare to get wet.
> —*Chinese proverb*

> **EXAMPLE:**
> I think this means if you travel, you have to accept whatever conditions you find.

If you are traveling, even a straw is heavy.
> —*English proverb*

If a donkey goes traveling, he doesn't come home a horse.
> —*U.S. proverb*

If you wish to be thoroughly misinformed about a country, consult a man who has lived there for thirty years and speaks the language like a native.
> —*George Bernard Shaw (Irish playwright, 1856–1950)*

If you reject the food, ignore the customs, fear the religion, and avoid the people, you might [as well] stay home. You are like a pebble thrown into water; you become wet on the surface, but you are never part of the water.
> —*James Michener (U.S. novelist, 1907–1997)*

Own only what you can carry with you: know language, know countries, know people. Let your memory be your travel bag.
> —*Alexander Solzhenitsyin (Russian novelist, 1918–)*

A journey of a thousand miles begins with the first step.
> —*Lao Tzu (Chinese philosopher, 6th cent., B.C.)*

11 WRITING

Work with a partner. Imagine that you are preparing a travel brochure for your city or town. Use factual conditional sentences and write tips for visitors. Compare your brochure with another pair's.

EXAMPLES:

If you enjoy swimming or boating, you should visit Ocean Park.

If you like to shop, Caterville has the biggest mall in this part of the country.

INFORMATION GAP FOR STUDENT B

Student B, look at the chart below. Answer your partner's questions. Ask your partner questions to complete the chart.

	Best Time to Go	**Currency**	**Time: When it's noon in New York . . .**
Caracas, Venezuela	December–April	bolívar	1:00 P.M.
Istanbul, Turkey	April–October	Turkish lira	
Rio de Janeiro, Brazil		real	
Seoul, South Korea	October–March		
Vancouver, Canada		Canadian dollar	
Moscow, Russia	May–September		8:00 P.M.

EXAMPLE:

A: If you travel to Caracas, what's the best time to go?

B: December through April.
What kind of currency do you need if you go there?

A: The bolívar.
When it's noon in New York, what time is it in Caracas?

When you are done, compare charts. Are they the same?

22 FACTUAL CONDITIONALS: FUTURE

GRAMMAR **IN CONTEXT**

BEFORE YOU READ   What are some issues that candidates for city mayor might discuss?

Two candidates are running for mayor of a large city. Read their statements from their campaign fliers.

DANIEL BAKER

Party:	Democrat
Occupation:	Mayor
Background:	City Clerk, State Assemblyman, attorney
Education:	Yale Law School, LL.B.;
	Howard University, B.S. cum laude

Four years ago, I promised to create a government that you could count on. Today, after four years as mayor of this great city, I am proud to say that we have come a long way. But the job is not finished. **If I am reelected, we will finish the work we started four years ago.**

My first priority is education. In the next ten years, there will be millions of new jobs in this country. **Many of those jobs could be filled by citizens of our city if we prepare them.** But **they won't be ready unless we improve our school system now.**

My second priority is housing. **It won't do any good to provide jobs if people continue to live in bad conditions.** We must rebuild housing in our city neighborhoods. My opponent talks about a "war on crime." I agree that violent crime is a problem. But **we're not going to solve the social problems in this city unless we house people better.**

If our city offers an educated work force, business will thrive here. This will provide more money to rebuild housing. **If our citizens have decent homes, then our neighborhoods will become healthy again.** These problems won't go away quickly. But **if we work together, we will solve them.** I urge everyone to get out and vote on election day. **Unless you vote, you will not have a say in the future of our great city.**

MAYORAL CANDIDATE
GABRIELA SOTO

Party: Republican
Occupation: City Comptroller
Background: District Attorney, lawyer
Education: U.C.L.A. Law School, LL.B.; U.S.C., B.A.

Today, street crime has made many people afraid to leave their homes. **If I am elected, I will give neighborhoods back to their citizens.** A lot of this violence is being committed by young offenders. My administration will say to them: **If you want to stay out of trouble, we will help you do that. But if you do the crime, you'll do the time. If you commit a violent crime, you will go to jail and serve your full sentence.**

If I become your mayor, I will put more police on the streets and set up a cooperative program between police and communities. Together we will fight for every street and every house, and together we will win. **This will be my first priority if I am elected.**

But **our young people won't avoid crime unless they have hope for their futures.** That's why my second priority as mayor will be to bring businesses back to our city. My opponent raised taxes as soon as he took office four years ago. As a result, many businesses left town. **If we lower taxes, they will return. If businesses return, our youth will have the hope of finding jobs.** And **if they have hope, they will not turn to a life of crime.**

I urge you to vote for me next Tuesday. **If I am elected, we'll hang out a sign:** "Open for business again."

GRAMMAR **PRESENTATION**
FACTUAL CONDITIONALS: FUTURE

AFFIRMATIVE STATEMENTS

IF CLAUSE: PRESENT	RESULT CLAUSE: FUTURE
If she **wins**,	she**'ll lower** taxes. she**'s going to fight** crime.

NEGATIVE STATEMENTS

IF CLAUSE: PRESENT	RESULT CLAUSE: FUTURE
If she **doesn't lower** taxes,	business **won't return**.

YES / NO QUESTIONS

IF CLAUSE: PRESENT	RESULT CLAUSE: FUTURE
If she **wins**,	**will** she **lower** taxes?
	is she **going to fight** crime?

SHORT ANSWERS

AFFIRMATIVE	
Yes, she	**will**.
	is.

SHORT ANSWERS

NEGATIVE	
No, she	**won't**.
	isn't.

WH- QUESTIONS

RESULT CLAUSE: FUTURE		IF CLAUSE: PRESENT
What	**will** she **do** **is** she **going to do**	if she **wins**?

NOTES

EXAMPLES

1. Use **future factual conditional** sentences to talk about what <u>will happen under certain conditions</u>. The *if* clause states the condition. The result clause states the probable or certain result.

Use the <u>simple present</u> in the *if* clause. Use the <u>future with *will* or *be going to*</u> in the result clause.

if clause   *result clause*
- ***If** Soto **wins**, she**'ll lower** taxes.*
  (It's a real possibility that Soto will win.)

- ***If** Baker **wins**, he**'ll improve** housing.*
- ***If** Baker **wins**, he**'s going to improve** housing.*

You can also use a **modal** in the result clause.	• If you want to vote, you ***must* register**.
▶ **BE CAREFUL!** Even though the *if* clause refers to the future, use the <u>simple present tense</u>.	• *If* she **wins**, she'll fight crime. NOT ~~If she will win . . .~~

2. You can begin conditional sentences with the *if* clause or the result clause. The meaning is the same.	• **If you vote for Baker,** you won't regret it. OR
▶ **BE CAREFUL!** Use a comma between the two clauses only when the *if* clause comes first.	• You won't regret it **if you vote for Baker**.

3. You can make either or both clauses <u>negative</u> in conditional sentences.	• If he wins, taxes will be higher. • If he **doesn't** win, taxes will be lower. • If he wins, taxes **won't** be lower. • If he **doesn't** win, taxes **won't** be higher.

4. *If* and *unless* can both be used in conditional sentences, but their meanings are very different. Use *unless* to state a <u>negative condition</u>.	• *If* Baker wins, the Democrats will remain in control. • *Unless* Baker wins, the Republicans will gain control. *(If Baker doesn't win, the Republicans will gain control.)*
Often, but not always, *unless* has the same meaning as *if . . . not*.	• *Unless* you vote, you won't have a say in the future of our city. OR • *If* you do*n't* vote, you won't have a say in the future of our city.

If they brought it, bring

FOCUSED PRACTICE

1 DISCOVER THE GRAMMAR

Match the conditions with the results.

Condition

h	**1.**	If Soto wins, she
k	**2.**	If we lower taxes, business people
b	**3.**	If companies move back to the city, there
g	**4.**	If young people want to stay out of trouble, the government
f	**5.**	If the education system improves, we
j	**6.**	Unless you register, you
c	**7.**	Unless you vote, you
d	**8.**	If the sanitation workers strike, there
e	**9.**	If crime decreases, this
l	**10.**	Unless young people have hope for the future, they
a	**11.**	If Baker wins, he
i	**12.**	Unless we work together on our problems, we

Result

a. will improve housing.

b. are going to be more jobs.

c. won't have a say in government.

d. will be more garbage in the streets.

e. will be a safer place to live.

f. will have an educated work force.

g. will help them.

h. will lower taxes.

i. aren't going to solve them.

j. won't be able to vote.

k. will move their companies back to the city.

l. won't stay out of trouble.

2 MEET THE PRESS

Complete this interview with another mayoral candidate, Herb Tresante. Use the correct form of the verbs in parentheses.

INTERVIEWER: Election day is just around the corner. Polls indicate that you have a pretty

good chance of winning. What's the first thing you ___'ll do___ if
1. (do)

you ___get___ elected?
2. (get)

TRESANTE: Well, it's been a long, hard campaign. If I ___win___, I
3. (win)

___will take___ a short vacation with my family.
4. (take)

INTERVIEWER: Sounds good. Where to?

TRESANTE: To be perfectly honest, I'd rather not say. If I ___become___ mayor, I
5. (become)

___will try___ to keep my private life private.
6. (try)

INTERVIEWER: I can understand that. Now, every election has a winner and a loser. What
_____will_____ you ___do___ if you ___lose___?
                                  7. (do)   8. (lose)

TRESANTE: Well, let's hope that won't happen. But, if I ___don't win___ this election,
                                                          9. (not win)
I 'll ___continue___ to be active in politics. Unless both parties
      10. (continue)
___cooperate___, this city ___will not be___ as great as it can be. If my
11. (cooperate)   12. (not be)
opponent ___accept___ my help, I ___will work___ to improve the
            13. (accept)   14. (work)
school system. And last, but not least, if the people ___do not elect___ me
                                                        15. (not elect)
to office this time, I ___will be___ back in four years to try again!
                          16. (be)

INTERVIEWER: How about a second term?

TRESANTE: If the voters ___want___ me for another four years, I
                          17. (want)
___will be___ back for sure!
   18. (be)

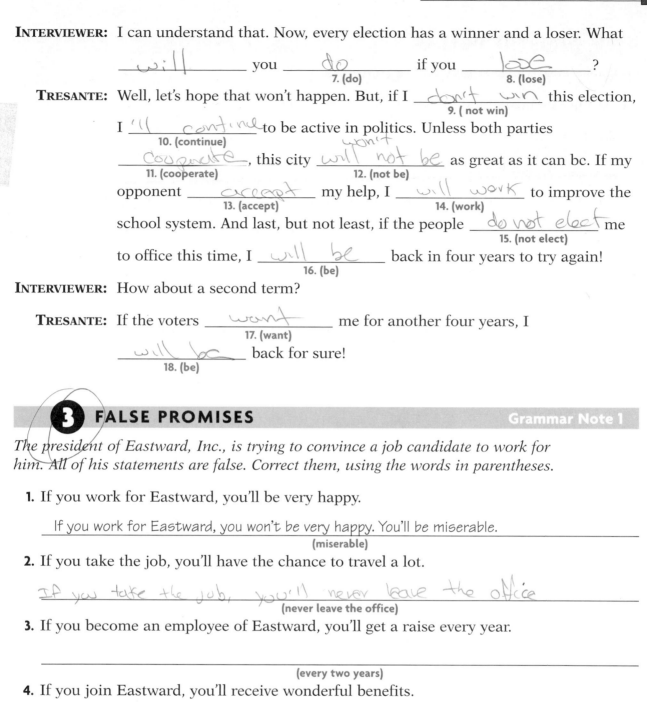

❸ FALSE PROMISES   Grammar Note 1

The president of Eastward, Inc., is trying to convince a job candidate to work for him. All of his statements are false. Correct them, using the words in parentheses.

1. If you work for Eastward, you'll be very happy.

  If you work for Eastward, you won't be very happy. You'll be miserable.
                              (miserable)

2. If you take the job, you'll have the chance to travel a lot.

  If you take the job, you'll never leave the office
                              (never leave the office)

3. If you become an employee of Eastward, you'll get a raise every year.

  _____
                              (every two years)

4. If you join Eastward, you'll receive wonderful benefits.

  _____
                              (terrible benefits)

5. If you come to Eastward, you'll have helpful co-workers.

  _____
                              (uncooperative)

6. If you accept Eastward's offer, it will be the best career move of your life.

  _____
                              (the worst)

4 AT THE POLLS

*Complete these conversations with **if** or **unless**.*

1. A: Oh, no. I can't find my voter registration card.

   B: That's OK. _____If_____ you don't have it, they'll look your name up in the

   registration book.

2. A: I've never voted before. I hope I can figure out how to use the voting machine.

   B: Don't worry. _____ you have trouble, they'll show you what to do.

3. A: I really didn't feel like coming out tonight.

   B: Me neither. But we won't have any say at all _____ we vote.

4. A: I've got to make a phone call. Would you mind holding my place in line?

   B: Sure. _____ it gets close to your turn, I'll come get you.

   A: Thanks.

5. A: Hi, Alicia. This is Manuel. I'm calling from the polling place. Where are you?

   B: I'm getting ready to leave now.

   A: Better hurry. They close the doors at nine o'clock. You won't get here in time

   _____ you leave right away.

6. A: Do you have the bus schedule? They don't come that frequently at this time.

   B: Stop worrying! _____ the bus doesn't come right away, I'll take a taxi.

7. A: Baker really supports education.

   B: _____ he wins, he'll improve the school system.

8. A: I really hope Soto wins.

   B: Me too. I'm going to be *very* unhappy _____ she loses.

   A: Well, it's going to be a close race. Keep your fingers crossed.

9. B: Why?

   A: _____ you cross your fingers, you'll have good luck.

   B: I didn't know you were superstitious.

5 EDITING

Read this journal entry. Find and correct six mistakes in the use of future factual conditionals. The first mistake is already corrected. (Don't forget to check commas.)

October 1

Should I campaign for student council president? I'll have to decide soon if I ~~wanted~~ ^{want} to

run. If I'll be busy campaigning, I won't have much time to study. That's a problem because

I'm not going to get into a good college if I get good grades this year. On the other hand,

there's so much to do in this school, and nothing is getting done if Todd Laker becomes

president again. A lot of people know that. But will I know what to do if I'll get the job?

Never mind. I'll deal with that problem, if I win.

6 WHAT IF . . .   **Grammar Notes 1 and 2**

Yukio Tamari is trying to decide whether to go to law school. She made a decision tree to help her decide. In the tree, arrows connect the conditions and the results. Write sentences about her decision. Use future factual conditional sentences.

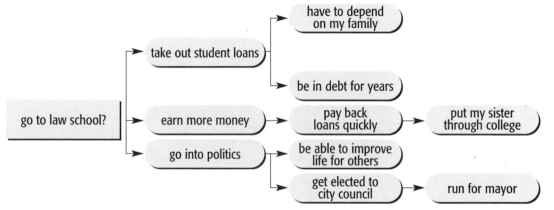

1. If I go to law school, I will take out student loans.

2. I'll be in debt for years if I take out student loans.

3. If I go to law school, I will go into politics.

4. I'll be able to improve life for others if I go into politics

5. If I go to law school, I will earn more money.

6. I will be able to put my sister through college if I earn more money.

7. I will run for mayor if I get elected to city council

8. I will be able to pay back loans quickly if I earn more money.

COMMUNICATION PRACTICE

7 LISTENING

 Gabriela Soto is talking about her political platform. Listen to the interview. Then read the list of issues. Listen again and check the things that Soto promises to do if she is elected.

1. ☑ hold neighborhood meetings
2. ☑ open recreation centers
3. ☐ close health centers at six o'clock *(until 9 pm)*
4. ☑ raise teachers' salaries
5. ☐ raise taxes *lower*
6. ☑ improve public transportation

8 SOLUTIONS

Work in pairs. Read these problems and think of possible solutions. Use **if**, **if . . . not**, *or* **unless**.

1. Your neighbors are always playing music so loud that you can't fall asleep.

   > **EXAMPLE:**
   > If they don't stop, I'll call the police.
   > Unless they stop, I'll call the landlord.
   > If they continue to bother me, I'll consider moving.

2. You've had a headache every day for a week. You can't concentrate.

3. You keep phoning your boyfriend or girlfriend, but there is no answer. It's now midnight.

4. You like your job, but you just found out that other workers are making much more money than you are.

5. You live in an apartment building. It's winter and the building hasn't had any heat for a week. You're freezing.

6. You're ten pounds overweight. You've been trying for months to lose weight, but so far you haven't lost a single pound.

7. You bought a radio in a local store. It doesn't work, but when you tried to return it, the salesclerk refused to take it back.

8. Your roommates don't clean up after they cook. You've already reminded them several times, but they always "forget."

9. You paid for a parking space near school or work. For the past week the same car has taken your space.

9 SUPERSTITIONS

Campaigning takes a lot of hard work, but luck is also important. Here are some superstitions about luck. Work in small groups and discuss similar superstitions that you know about.

If you cross your fingers, you'll have good luck.

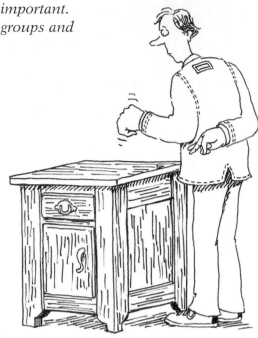

> **EXAMPLE:**
> In Germany, people believe that if you press your thumbs, you will have good luck.

If you touch blue, your dreams will come true.

If you break a mirror, you will have seven years of bad luck.

If you put on a piece of clothing inside out, you will have good luck.

If your palm itches, you're going to find some money soon.

With your group, make a list of superstitions. Use the following ideas or your own.

getting married	knocking on wood
finding money	sneezing
losing money	whistling
having good luck	dropping or spilling something
having bad luck	taking the last piece of food

> **EXAMPLE:**
> If you take the last piece of food on a plate, you won't get married.

Share your list of superstitions with the whole class.

10 WRITING

Imagine you are running for the position of class or school president. Write a short speech. Include five campaign promises. In small groups, give your speeches and elect a candidate. Then hold a general class election.

> **EXAMPLE:**
> If I become school president, I will buy ten new computers.
> If you elect me, I'll . . .

23 UNREAL CONDITIONALS: PRESENT

GRAMMAR IN CONTEXT

BEFORE YOU READ   What kind of story is a fairy tale? What is the title of a famous fairy tale from your culture?

Read this version of a famous fairy tale.

The Fisherman and His Wife

Once upon a time there was a poor fisherman and his wife who lived in a pigsty near the sea. Every day the man went to fish. One day, after waiting a very long time, he caught a very big fish. To his surprise, the fish spoke and said, "Please let me live. I'm not a regular fish. **If you knew my real identity, you wouldn't kill me.** I'm an enchanted prince."

"Don't worry. I won't kill you," said the kind-hearted fisherman. With these words, he threw the fish back into the clear water, and went home to his wife.

"Husband," said the wife, "didn't you catch anything today?"

"I caught a fish, but it said it was an enchanted prince, so I let it go." *enchanted*

"You mean you didn't wish for anything?" asked the wife.

"No," said the fisherman. "What do I need to wish for?"

"Just look around you," said the wife. "We live in a pigsty. **I wish we had a nice little cottage. If we had a cottage, I would be a lot happier.** You saved the prince's life. Go back and ask him for it." *cavech*

"I'm not going to ask for a cottage! **If I asked for a cottage, the fish would be angry.**" But in the end, the fisherman was more afraid of his wife's anger.

When he got to the sea, it was all green and yellow. **"My wife wishes we had a cottage,"** said the fisherman. "Just go on back," said the fish. "She already has it."

When he returned home, the fisherman found his wife sitting outside a lovely little cottage. The kitchen was filled with food and all types of cooking utensils. Outside was a little garden with vegetables, fruit trees, hens, and ducks.

Things were fine for a week or two. Then the wife said, "This cottage is much too crowded. **I wish we lived in a bigger house. If we lived in a big stone castle, I would be much happier.** Go and ask the fish for it."

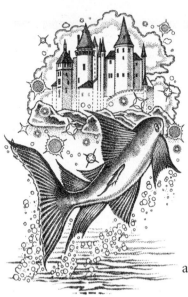

The fisherman didn't want to go, but he did. When he got to the sea, it was dark blue and gray. **"My wife wishes we lived in a big stone castle,"** he said to the fish.

"Just go on back. She's standing in front of the door," said the fish.

When he returned home, the fisherman found his wife on the steps of a great big stone castle. The inside was filled with beautiful gold furniture, chandeliers, and carpets, and there were servants everywhere.

The next morning the wife woke up and said, **"I wish I were King of all this land."**

"What would you do if you were King?" asked her husband.

"If I were King, I would own all this land. Go on back and ask the fish for it."

This time, the sea was all blackish gray, and the water was rough and smelled terrible. "What does she want now?" asked the fish.

"She wants to be King," said the embarrassed fisherman.

"Just go on back. She already is."

When the fisherman returned home, he found an enormous palace. Everything inside was made of marble and pure gold, and it was surrounded by soldiers with drums and trumpets. His wife was seated on a throne, and he said to her, "How nice for you that you are King. Now we won't need to wish for anything else."

But his wife was not satisfied. **"If I were Emperor, I would be much happier,"** she said. "I am King and I command you to go back and ask the fish to make me Emperor."

Reluctantly, the fisherman went back to the fish, and again the wish was granted. Next, his wife wanted to be Pope, and that wish, too, was granted. "Wife, now be satisfied," said the fisherman. "You're Pope. You can't be anything more."

48

The wife, however, wasn't convinced. She kept thinking and thinking about what more she could be. **"I wish I were like the Lord of the universe,"** she finally said. **"If I were like the Lord, I could make the sun rise and set.** Then **I would be much happier.** Go right now and tell the fish that I want to be like the Lord."

"Oh, no," said the fisherman. "The fish can't do that. **If I were you, I wouldn't ask for anything else."** But his wife got so furious that the poor fisherman ran back to the fish. There was a terrible storm, and the sea was pitch black with waves as high as mountains. "Well, what does she want now?" asked the fish.

"She wishes she were like the Lord of the universe," said the fisherman.

"Just go on back. She's sitting in the pigsty again."

And they are still sitting there today. ❋

GRAMMAR **PRESENTATION**
UNREAL CONDITIONALS: PRESENT

AFFIRMATIVE STATEMENTS		
IF CLAUSE: SIMPLE PAST		**RESULT CLAUSE: *WOULD* + BASE FORM OF VERB**
If she	**had** money, **were*** rich,	she **would live** in a palace.

*Note that *were* is used for all persons of *be*.

NEGATIVE STATEMENTS		
IF CLAUSE: SIMPLE PAST		**RESULT CLAUSE: *WOULD NOT* + BASE FORM OF VERB**
If she	**didn't have** money, **weren't** rich,	she **would not live** in a palace.

CONTRACTIONS		
I would	=	**I'd**
you would	=	**you'd**
he would	=	**he'd**
she would	=	**she'd**
we would	=	**we'd**
they would	=	**they'd**
would not	=	**wouldn't**

YES / NO QUESTIONS			SHORT ANSWERS	SHORT ANSWERS
RESULT CLAUSE	**IF CLAUSE**		**AFFIRMATIVE**	**NEGATIVE**
Would you **live** here	**if** you	**had** money? **were** rich?	**Yes**, I **would**.	**No**, I **wouldn't**.

WH- QUESTIONS		
RESULT CLAUSE	**IF CLAUSE**	
What **would** you **do**	**if** you	**had** money? **were** rich?

NOTES	**EXAMPLES**

1. Use **present unreal conditional** sentences to talk about <u>unreal, untrue, imagined, or impossible conditions and their results</u>.

The *if* clause presents the unreal condition. The result clause presents the unreal result of that condition.

           if clause   result clause
- *If* I **lived** in a palace, I **would give** parties all the time.
(But I don't live in a palace, so I don't give parties.)

           if clause   result clause
- *If* I **had** more time, I **would read** fairy tales to my children.
(But I don't have time, so I don't read them fairy tales.)

---

2. Use the <u>simple past tense</u> in the *if* clause. Use **_would_** + base form of the verb in the result clause.

▶ **BE CAREFUL!**

    a. The *if* clause uses the <u>simple past</u> tense form, but <u>the meaning is not past</u>.

    b. Don't use *would* in the *if* clause in present unreal conditional sentences.

    c. Use **_were_** for <u>all persons</u> when the verb in the *if* clause is a form of *be*.

    USAGE NOTE: You will sometimes hear native speakers use *was* in the *if* clause. However, many people think that this is not correct.

- *If* they **had** money, they **wouldn't live** in a pigsty.

- *If* I **had** more money *now*, I would take a trip around the world.

- *If* she **knew** the answer, she would tell you.
NOT ~~If she would know the answer . . .~~

- *If* I **were** King, I would make you prime minister.
NOT ~~If I was King . . .~~

---

3. If the result is not certain, use **_might_** or **_could_** in the result clause to express <u>possibility</u>.

You can also use **_could_** in the result clause to express <u>ability</u>.

- If I had time, I **_might / could_ read** more.
(It's possible I would read more often.)

- If you knew German, you **_could_ translate** this story for me.

(continued on next page)

4. Remember that you can begin conditional sentences with the *if* clause or the result clause. The meaning is the same.

▶ **BE CAREFUL!** Use a comma between the two clauses only when the *if* clause comes first.

- **If I had more money,** I would move.

  OR

- I would move **if I had more money.**

---

5. Remember that you can make either or both clauses <u>negative</u> in conditional sentences.

- If I caught a fish, I would be happy.
- If I **didn't** catch a fish, I would be unhappy.
- If I caught a fish, I **wouldn't** be unhappy.
- If I **didn't** catch a fish, I **wouldn't** be happy.

---

6. Statements beginning with *If I were you, . . .* are often used to <u>give advice</u>.

- **If I were you,** I wouldn't ask the fish for anything else. He could get angry.

---

7. Use *wish* followed by a verb in the **simple past tense** to talk about <u>things that you want to be true now, but that are not true</u>.

Note that after *wish*, **were** is used instead of *was*.

Use **could** or **would** after *wish*. Don't use *can* or *will*.

- I **wish** I **lived** in a castle.
  (I don't live in a castle, but I want to live in one.)
- I **wish** we **had** a yacht.
  (We don't have a yacht, but I want one.)
- I **wish** I *were* a child again.
  NOT ~~I wish I was a child again.~~
- I **wish** I *could* buy a car.
  NOT ~~I wish I can buy a car.~~
- I **wish** she *would* call tomorrow.
  NOT ~~I wish she will call tomorrow.~~

FOCUSED PRACTICE

1 DISCOVER THE GRAMMAR

Read the numbered statement. Then, based on the information in the statement, decide if sentences a and b are True (T) or False (F).

1. If I had time, I would read fairy tales in English.

   ___F___ **a.** I have time.

   ___F___ **b.** I'm going to read fairy tales in English.

2. If it weren't so cold, I would go fishing.

   ___T___ **a.** It's cold.

   ___F___ **b.** I'm going fishing.

3. If I caught an enchanted fish, I would make three wishes.

   ___F___ **a.** I believe I'm going to catch an enchanted fish.

   ___F___ **b.** I'm going to make three wishes.

4. If I had three wishes, I wouldn't ask for a palace.

   ___F___ **a.** I have three wishes.

   ___T___ **b.** I don't want a palace.

5. If my house were too small, I would try to find a bigger one.

   ___T___ **a.** My house is big enough.

   ___T___ **b.** I'm not looking for a bigger house right now.

6. If we won the lottery, we would buy a new car.

   ___F___ **a.** We recently won the lottery.

   ___T___ **b.** We want a new car.

7. If we didn't earn enough money, I would train for a better job.

   ___F___ **a.** We don't earn enough money.

   ___F___ **b.** I'm training for a better job.

8. Your friend tells you, "If I were you, I wouldn't change jobs."

   ___T___ **a.** Your friend is giving you advice.

   ___T___ **b.** Your friend thinks you shouldn't change jobs.

9. I wish I were a princess.

   ___F___ **a.** I'm a princess.

   ___T___ **b.** I want to be a princess.

10. I wish I lived in a big house.

    ___T___ **a.** I want to live in a big house.

    ___T___ **b.** I don't live in a big house.

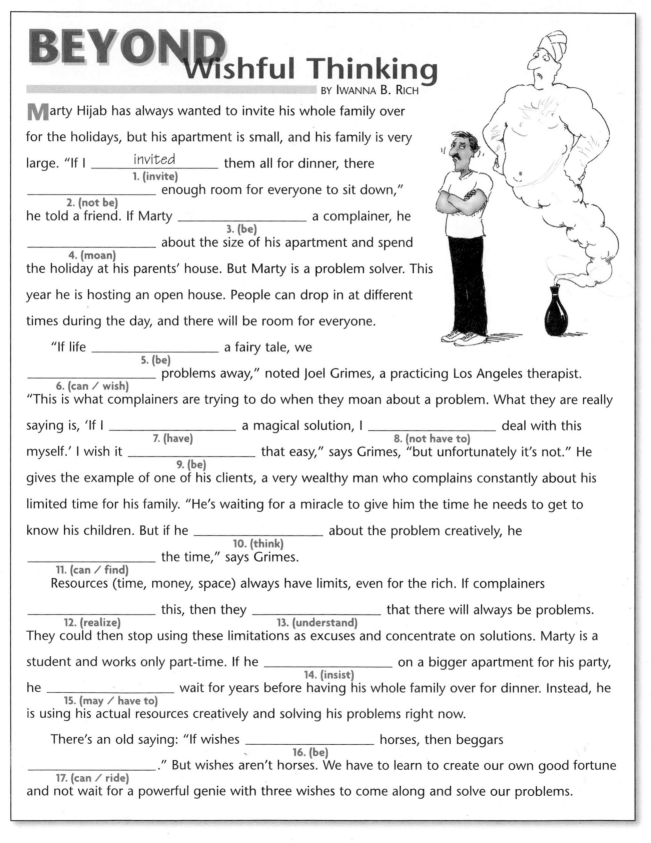

2 ABRACADABRA?

Complete this article from a popular psychology magazine. Use the correct form of the verbs in parentheses.

BEYOND Wishful Thinking

BY IWANNA B. RICH

Marty Hijab has always wanted to invite his whole family over for the holidays, but his apartment is small, and his family is very large. "If I _____*invited*_____ them all for dinner, there
1. (invite)

_____ enough room for everyone to sit down,"
2. (not be)

he told a friend. If Marty _____ a complainer, he
3. (be)

_____ about the size of his apartment and spend
4. (moan)

the holiday at his parents' house. But Marty is a problem solver. This year he is hosting an open house. People can drop in at different times during the day, and there will be room for everyone.

"If life _____ a fairy tale, we
5. (be)

_____ problems away," noted Joel Grimes, a practicing Los Angeles therapist.
6. (can / wish)

"This is what complainers are trying to do when they moan about a problem. What they are really

saying is, 'If I _____ a magical solution, I _____ deal with this
7. (have)   8. (not have to)

myself.' I wish it _____ that easy," says Grimes, "but unfortunately it's not." He
9. (be)

gives the example of one of his clients, a very wealthy man who complains constantly about his

limited time for his family. "He's waiting for a miracle to give him the time he needs to get to

know his children. But if he _____ about the problem creatively, he
10. (think)

_____ the time," says Grimes.
11. (can / find)

Resources (time, money, space) always have limits, even for the rich. If complainers

_____ this, then they _____ that there will always be problems.
12. (realize)   13. (understand)

They could then stop using these limitations as excuses and concentrate on solutions. Marty is a

student and works only part-time. If he _____ on a bigger apartment for his party,
14. (insist)

he _____ wait for years before having his whole family over for dinner. Instead, he
15. (may / have to)

is using his actual resources creatively and solving his problems right now.

There's an old saying: "If wishes _____ horses, then beggars
16. (be)

_____." But wishes aren't horses. We have to learn to create our own good fortune
17. (can / ride)

and not wait for a powerful genie with three wishes to come along and solve our problems.

3 MAKING EXCUSES

In his practice, psychologist Joel Grimes hears all types of excuses from his clients. Rewrite these excuses, using present unreal conditional sentences.

1. I'm so busy. That's why I don't read bedtime stories to my little girl.

   If I weren't so busy, I would read bedtime stories to my little girl.

2. My husband's not ambitious. That's why he doesn't ask for a raise.

   _____

3. I'm not in shape. That's why I don't play sports.

   _____

4. I don't have enough time. That's why I'm not planning to study for the exam.

   _____

5. I'm too old. That's why I'm not going back to school.

   _____

6. My boss doesn't explain things properly. That's why I can't do my job.

   _____

7. I'm not good at math. That's why I don't balance my checkbook.

   _____

8. I feel nervous all the time. That's why I can't stop smoking.

   _____

4 THE FISH'S WISHES

Remember the fish from the fairy tale on pages 336–337? Now read his regrets. Rewrite them with **wish**.

1. I'm a fish. I wish I weren't a fish. _____

2. I'm not a handsome prince. _____

3. I live in the sea. _____

4. I don't live in a castle. _____

5. I have to swim all day long. _____

(continued on next page)

6. I am not married to a princess. _____

7. The fisherman comes here every day. _____

8. His wife always wants more. _____

9. She isn't satisfied. _____

10. They don't leave me alone. _____

⑤ WHAT IF?   Grammar Notes 1–4

Marty is having his open-house holiday party. His nieces and nephews are playing a fantasy question game. Complete their questions with the following words.

1. What / you / do / if / you / be a millionaire?

   What would you do if you were a millionaire?

2. What / you / do / if / you / be the leader of this country?

   _____

3. How / you / feel / if / you / never need to sleep?

   _____

4. What / you / do / if / you / have more free time?

   _____

5. What / you / do / if / you / can swim like a fish?

   _____

6. What / you / do / if / you / not have to work?

   _____

7. Where / you / travel / if / you / have a ticket for anywhere in the world?

   _____

8. If / you / can build anything / what / it / be?

   _____

9. If / you / can meet a famous person / who / you / want to meet?

   _____

6 EDITING

Read part of a book report that Marty's niece wrote. Find and correct six mistakes in the use of the present unreal conditional. The first mistake is already corrected.

NAME: Laila Hijab

CLASS: English 4

The Disappearance

What would happen to the women if all the men in the
                  disappeared
world ~~would disappear~~? What would happen to the men when
there were no women? Philip Wiley's 1951 science-fiction
novel, *The Disappearance*, addresses these intriguing
questions.

According to Wiley, if men and women live in different
worlds, the results would be catastrophic. Wiley thinks
that men are too aggressive to survive on their own. If
women didn't control them, men will start more wars. He
also believes that women wouldn't have the technological
skills to survive in their own world. If men aren't there
to pump gas and run the businesses, women wouldn't be able
to manage.

Many people disagree with Wiley's visions. In fact, they
think the book is sexist. They don't think men are more
warlike than women, and they don't believe that women are
more helpless than men. I think if men and women learned to
cooperate more, the world will be a much better place.

COMMUNICATION PRACTICE

7 LISTENING

You are going to listen to a modern fairy tale about Cindy, a clever young girl, and a toad. Before you listen, read the statements. Then listen again and mark each statement **True (T)** *or* **False (F)**.

__F__ **1.** Cindy wishes she had a new soccer ball.

_____ **2.** The toad wishes Cindy would marry him.

_____ **3.** If Cindy married the toad, he would become a prince.

_____ **4.** Cindy wishes she could become a beautiful princess.

_____ **5.** If Cindy became a princess, she'd have plenty of time to study science.

_____ **6.** The toad doesn't know how to use his powers to help himself.

_____ **7.** Cindy wants to become a scientist and help the prince.

_____ **8.** Cindy and the prince get married and live happily ever after.

8 JUST IMAGINE

Work in small groups. Answer the questions in Exercise 5. Discuss your answers with your classmates.

EXAMPLE:
A: What would you do if you were a millionaire?
B: If I were a millionaire, I would donate half my money to charity.

9 IF I WERE YOU . . .

Work in pairs. You have a problem. Your classmate gives advice beginning with **If I were you, I would / wouldn't . . .**

1. You need $500 to pay this month's rent. You only have $300.

EXAMPLE:
If I were you, I'd try to borrow the money.

2. You are lonely. You work at home and never meet new people.

3. You never have an opportunity to practice English outside of class.

4. You have been invited to dinner. You know that the main dish is going to be shrimp. You hate shrimp.

Add problems of your own. Ask your partner for advice.

5. _____

6. _____

7. _____

⑩ JUST THREE WISHES

In fairy tales, people are often granted three wishes. Imagine that you had just three wishes. What would they be? Write them down. Discuss them with a classmate.

EXAMPLE:
I wish I were famous.
I wish I spoke perfect English.
I wish I knew how to fly a plane.

There is an old saying: "Be careful what you wish for; it may come true." Look at your wishes again. Discuss what negative results might happen if they came true.

EXAMPLE:
If I were famous, I would have no free time. I wouldn't have a private life . . .

⑪ WRITING

Reread the book report on page 345. Does Wiley believe men and women should live in separate worlds? What are his arguments? Do you agree with him? Write two paragraphs that support your opinion.

EXAMPLE:
I don't think men and women should live in separate societies, but sometimes I think that boys and girls would learn better if they went to separate schools. For example, when I was in middle school, boys and girls were embarrassed to make mistakes in front of each other . . .

24 UNREAL CONDITIONALS: PAST

GRAMMAR IN CONTEXT

BEFORE YOU READ   Look at the photographs. What do you think the movie is about? What does the reviewer think of the movie? How long is it?

Read this video review from the entertainment section of a newspaper.

Section 5/**ENTERTAINMENT**   4A

Best Bets for Holiday Viewing

It's A Wonderful Life
(1946)

Rating: ★★★★ out of ★★★★
Director: Frank Capra
Producer: Frank Capra
Screenplay: Frank Capra, Frances Goodrich, Albert Hacket, and Jo Swerling
Stars: James Stewart, Donna Reed, Lionel Barrymore, Thomas Mitchell, Henry Travers
Running Time: 129 m
Parental Guidelines: suitable for whole family

What would have happened if you had never been born? George Bailey learns the answer in Frank Capra's great movie classic *It's a Wonderful Life.*

When the movie opens, George is standing on a bridge contemplating suicide. Throughout his life, he has sacrificed his dreams in order to help other people. **He could have gone to college if the family business hadn't needed him. He would have traveled around the world** instead of remaining in his hometown of Bedford Falls. Now, facing bankruptcy and a possible jail sentence, George decides to end his life by jumping into the river. Enter Clarence, an angel sent to help him. Clarence jumps into the water first, certain that, as always, George would put aside his own problems in order to rescue someone else.

Safely back on land, George tells his guardian angel, "I suppose **it would have been better if I had never been born at all.**" "You've got your wish: You've never been born," responds Clarence.

(continued on next page)

Best Bets for Holiday Viewing *(continued)*

George (seated) and his guardian angel

Clarence then teaches George a hard lesson. In a series of painful episodes, he shows him what **life would have been like in Bedford Falls without George Bailey**. George goes back to the site of his mother's home. He finds, instead, an old, depressing boarding house. **If George had not supported his mother, she would have become an embittered, overworked boarding house owner**. George's own home is a ruin, and his wife Mary is living a sad life of isolation. Each scene is more disturbing than the last, until finally we end in a graveyard. We see the grave of George's little brother Harry. **If George hadn't been alive, he couldn't have saved his younger brother Harry's life.**

Harry would have drowned in a childhood sledding accident. And **Harry would have never grown up to be a war hero**, saving the lives of hundreds of soldiers. "Harry wasn't there to save them because you weren't there to save Harry," explains Clarence. "You see, George, you really had a wonderful life. Don't you see what a mistake it would be to throw it away?"

The ending of the movie delivers a heartwarming holiday message. *It's a Wonderful Life* shows us the importance of each person's life and how each of our lives touches those of others. We see through George's eyes how **the lives of those around him would have been different if he hadn't known them**.

This movie is highly recommended for the whole family.

George is reunited with his family

GRAMMAR **PRESENTATION**
UNREAL CONDITIONALS: PAST

AFFIRMATIVE STATEMENTS	
IF CLAUSE: PAST PERFECT	RESULT CLAUSE: *WOULD HAVE* + PAST PARTICIPLE
If I **had had** money,	I **would have moved** away.

NEGATIVE STATEMENTS	
IF CLAUSE: PAST PERFECT	RESULT CLAUSE: *WOULD NOT HAVE* + PAST PARTICIPLE
If George **had not stayed** home,	he **would not have married** Mary.

YES / NO QUESTIONS		SHORT ANSWERS	SHORT ANSWERS
RESULT CLAUSE	IF CLAUSE	AFFIRMATIVE	NEGATIVE
Would you **have left**	if you **had had** money?	**Yes, I would have.**	**No, I wouldn't have.**

WH- QUESTIONS		CONTRACTIONS	
RESULT CLAUSE	IF CLAUSE	would have	= **would've**
What **would** you **have done**	if you **had had** money?	would not have	= **wouldn't have**

NOTES

EXAMPLES

1. Use **past unreal conditional sentences** to talk about <u>past unreal, untrue, or imagined conditions and their unreal results</u>. These sentences are used to describe situations that never happened.

As in present unreal conditional sentences, the *if* clause presents the unreal condition, and the result clause presents the unreal result of that condition.

if clause   result clause
- ***If*** he **had died** young, he **wouldn't have had** children.
  (*But he didn't die young, so he had children.*)

- ***If*** George **hadn't been born**, many people's lives **would have been** worse.
  (*But George was born, so people's lives were better.*)

2. Use the <u>past perfect</u> in the *if* clause. Use <u>***would have***</u> + <u>past participle</u> in the result clause.

USAGE NOTE: Sometimes native speakers use *would have* in the *if* clause. However, many people think that this is not correct.

- *If* the film **had won** an Academy Award, it **would have become** famous right away.

- *If* I **had owned** a VCR, I would have watched the movie.
  NOT ~~If I would have owned . . .~~

---

3. If the result is not certain, use ***might have*** or ***could have*** in the result clause to express <u>possibility</u>.

You can also use ***could have*** in the result clause to express <u>ability</u>.

- If George had gone to college, he ***might have*** become an architect.

- If George had become an architect, he ***could have*** designed bridges.

---

4. Remember that you can begin conditional sentences with the *if* clause or the result clause. The meaning is the same.

▶ **BE CAREFUL!** Use a comma between the two clauses only when the *if* clause comes first.

- **If he had won a million dollars,** he would have traveled to China.

  OR

- He would have traveled to China **if he had won a million dollars**.

---

5. Remember that you can make either or both clauses <u>negative</u> in conditional sentences.

- If it had rained, I would've stayed.
- If it **hadn't** rained, I would've left.
- If it had rained, I **wouldn't** have left.
- If it **hadn't** rained, I **wouldn't** have stayed.

---

6. Past unreal conditionals are often used to <u>express regret</u> about what really happened in the past.

- If I **had known** Mary was in town, I **would have invited** her to the party. *(I regret that I didn't invite her.)*

---

7. You can also use ***wish*** followed by a verb in the **past perfect** to <u>express regret or sadness about things in the past</u> that you wanted to happen, but didn't.

- George *wishes* he **had studied** architecture. *(He didn't study architecture, and now he thinks that was a mistake.)*

FOCUSED PRACTICE

1 DISCOVER THE GRAMMAR

Read the numbered statement. Then, based on the information in the statement, decide if sentences a *and* b *are* **True (T)** *or* **False (F)**.

1. If I had had time, I would have watched *It's a Wonderful Life*.

   ___T___ **a.** I didn't have time to watch *It's a Wonderful Life*.

   ___F___ **b.** I watched *It's a Wonderful Life*.

2. I would have taped the movie if my VCR hadn't broken.

   _____ **a.** I taped the movie.

   _____ **b.** My VCR broke.

3. If George Bailey hadn't been depressed, he wouldn't have wanted to jump off the bridge.

   _____ **a.** George was depressed.

   _____ **b.** George wanted to jump off the bridge.

4. If George hadn't saved his brother, his brother wouldn't have become a war hero.

   _____ **a.** George didn't save his brother's life.

   _____ **b.** George's brother became a war hero.

5. George wouldn't have met Mary if he hadn't gone to his brother's graduation party.

   _____ **a.** George met Mary.

   _____ **b.** George didn't go to the party.

6. George would have been happy if he had liked his job.

   _____ **a.** George wasn't happy.

   _____ **b.** George liked his job.

7. George says, "I wish I had traveled around the world."

   _____ **a.** George feels sad that he hasn't traveled around the world.

   _____ **b.** George has traveled around the world.

2 GEORGE'S THOUGHTS   Grammar Notes 1 and 2

Complete George's thoughts about the past. Use the correct form of the words in parentheses.

1. I didn't go into business with my friend Sam. If I ____had gone____ into business
   (go)
   with him, I ___would have become___ a success.
   (become)

2. I couldn't go into the army because I was deaf in one ear. I _____
   (go)
   into the army if I _____ my hearing in that ear.
   (not lose)

3. Mary and I weren't able to go on a honeymoon. We _____ away if my
   $\underset{\text{(can / go)}}{}$

   father _____ sick.
   $\underset{\text{(not get)}}{}$

4. My uncle lost $8,000 of the company's money. I _____ so desperate if
   $\underset{\text{(not feel)}}{}$

   he _____ the money.
   $\underset{\text{(find)}}{}$

5. I'm so unhappy. I wish I _____ never _____ born.
   $\underset{\text{(be)}}{}$

6. Clarence showed me how the world would look without me. I _____
   $\underset{\text{(not know)}}{}$

   that I was so important if Clarence _____ me.
   $\underset{\text{(not show)}}{}$

7. If I _____ my brother, he _____ all those lives.
   $\underset{\text{(not rescue)}}{}$ $\underset{\text{(not save)}}{}$

8. My old boss once almost made a terrible mistake. If I _____ him, he
   $\underset{\text{(not help)}}{}$

   _____ to jail.
   $\underset{\text{(go)}}{}$

9. Mary _____ happy if she _____ me.
   $\underset{\text{(not be)}}{}$ $\underset{\text{(not meet)}}{}$

10. Many people _____ buy homes if we _____ in
    $\underset{\text{(not be able to)}}{}$ $\underset{\text{(not stay)}}{}$

    business.

11. Life here really _____ different if I _____.
    $\underset{\text{(be)}}{}$ $\underset{\text{(not live)}}{}$

❸ REGRETS AND WISHES   Grammar Note 7

These people in the movie feel bad about some things. Read their regrets. Then write their wishes.

1. **Clarence (the angel):** I wasn't a first-class angel then. I didn't have much self-confidence.

   I wish I had been a first-class angel then.

   I wish I had had more self-confidence.

2. **Mr. Gower (George's childhood employer):** I hit little George when he was trying to help me. I wasn't nice to him.

   _____

   _____

3. **George:** My father had a heart attack. I had to stay and run the business.

   _____

   _____

(continued on next page)

4. Mary (George's wife): We weren't able to go on a honeymoon. We needed the money to save the business.

_____

_____

5. Mr. Potter (the town villain): I wasn't able to trick George out of his business. He didn't accept my offer to buy his business.

_____

_____

6. Billy (George's uncle): I lost $8,000. George got into trouble with the law because of me.

_____

_____

7. George's daughter: Daddy was upset about the business. He yelled at us on Christmas Eve.

_____

_____

8. George's friends: We didn't know about George's troubles earlier. We didn't help him immediately.

_____

_____

4 **THE LOST WALLET** Grammar Notes 1–3

In It's a Wonderful Life, *George's uncle loses $8,000. Mean Mr. Potter finds it and doesn't give it back. Complete this conversation about a lost wallet. Use the correct form of the verbs in parentheses and short answers.*

EMILY: Did you hear what happened to Lauren? She was walking down the street and

found a wallet with just a hundred dollar bill and a library card.

DIANE: Did she call the owner?

EMILY: If she _____ had had _____ the phone number, she _____, of

1. (have)   2. (call)

course, but the library card only had the person's name.

DIANE: Well, what did she do?

EMILY: She took it to the police.

DIANE: Oh, I _____ it to the police if I _____ it.
      3. (not take)   4. (find)

EMILY: Why not? What _____ you _____ if
                                                                    5. (do)

   you _____ the wallet?
              6. (find)

DIANE: I _____ to find the owner myself.
              7. (try)

EMILY: How? _____ you _____ a notice in the
                                            8. (put)

   newspaper?

DIANE: No, I _____. That would've been foolish. After all, anyone
                        9.

   _____ it.
       10. (can / answer)

EMILY: Well, it _____ easy if there _____
                        11. (be)   12. (be)

   more identification in the wallet. But there was only the person's name on the card.

DIANE: Well, I _____ in the phone book.
                        13. (look)

EMILY: She did look in the phone book. The name wasn't there. At least now that the

   police have it, the owner can try to get it back.

5 EDITING

*Read this journal entry. Find and correct six mistakes in the use of the unreal
conditional. The first mistake is already corrected.*

December 20

The police returned my wallet! And the money was still there!

If I wouldn't have gotten the money back, it would have been a

sad Christmas for us. Jamie would had felt terribly disappointed

if I hadn't bought him some new toys. And Chris would have

been frantic if we can't paid our bills on time. I wish the police

gave me the address of the woman who found my wallet. If I had

knew where she lived, I would of sent her a special holiday gift.

COMMUNICATION PRACTICE

6 LISTENING

Some friends are discussing a party. Listen to their short conversations. Then listen again and circle the letter of the sentence you heard.

1. a. If I had her number, I would call her.

  (b.) If I'd had her number, I would've called her.

2. a. I would've invited him if he'd been in town.

  b. I wouldn't have invited him if he'd been in town.

3. a. If he'd changed jobs, he would've gotten the same benefits.

  b. If he'd changed jobs, he wouldn't have gotten the same benefits.

4. a. I liked it better on a big screen.

  b. I would've liked it better on a big screen.

5. a. I wish David had invited her.

  b. I wish David hadn't invited her.

6. a. I would have.

  b. I wouldn't have.

7. a. If I'd invited Holly, I would've invited Greg.

  b. If I'd invited Holly, I wouldn't have invited Greg.

8. a. If the party had been on a Saturday, they could've come.

  b. If the party hadn't been on a Saturday, they could've come.

7 WHAT WOULD YOU HAVE DONE?

Read the following situations. In small groups discuss what you would have done for each situation.

1. George was going to go to jail. He had no money. He tried to kill himself.

> **EXAMPLE:**
> I would have tried to borrow the money. I wouldn't have tried to kill myself.

2. A man was walking down the street when he found ten $100 bills lying on the ground. There was no one else around. He picked them up and put them in his pocket.

3. A woman came home late and found her apartment door unlocked. She was sure she had locked it. No one else had the keys. She went inside.

4. A teenage boy was walking home when he saw two men fighting. One had a knife. The other was screaming "Help!" The teenager ran away.

8 **IF ONLY . . .**

With a partner discuss a situation in your life that you have regrets about.
Describe the situation and talk about what you wish had happened and why.

EXAMPLE:

Someone asked me to go to a party the night before a test. I didn't like
the course, and I didn't feel like studying, so I decided to go to the party.
The next day, I failed the test, and I had to repeat the course. I wish I hadn't
gone to the party. If I had stayed home, I would have studied for the test. If
I had been prepared, I would have passed.

9 **LIFE WITHOUT GEORGE**

Work in pairs. Look at the pictures. They show life with George Bailey and how
life would have been without him. Discuss the pictures.

Life with George: **Life without George:**

1.

EXAMPLE:

If George hadn't lived, mean Mr. Potter would've owned the town. They would've
called the town Pottersville, not Bedford Falls. The town wouldn't have been . . .

2.

(continued on next page)

Life with George:

Life without George:

3.

Mary

Mary

4.

Mr. Gower

Mr. Gower

5.

George's mother

George's mother

⑩ WRITING

If you hadn't been born, what would have been different for your family, friends, teammates, or community? Choose two areas of your life to discuss and write a paragraph about all the things that would have been different.

EXAMPLE:

Two important areas of my life are my family and my friends. I am an only child, so if I hadn't been born, my parents would have been sad. They wanted a child very much. If they hadn't had one of their own, they might have . . .

REVIEW OR SELFTEST

I. *Circle the letter of the correct word(s) to complete each sentence.*

1. I _____ late for work if the bus doesn't arrive soon.
   (A) am   (C) 'll be
   (B) was   (D) 've been

   A B Ⓒ D

2. I _____ a flight attendant if I didn't get airsick.
   (A) would become   (C) become
   (B) became   (D) had become

   A B C D

3. What do you do when your bus _____ late?
   (A) were   (C) would be
   (B) is   (D) had been

   A B C D

4. If the teacher cancels class today, I _____ you.
   (A) have joined   (C) 'll join
   (B) could have joined   (D) join

   A B C D

5. This flight is full. _____ someone gives up a seat, you won't get on this flight today.
   (A) If   (C) When
   (B) Unless   (D) Where

   A B C D

6. If you _____ early enough, we can't save a seat for you.
   (A) 'll check in   (C) don't check in
   (B) check in   (D) have checked in

   A B C D

7. If I hadn't been fascinated with flying, I _____ a pilot.
   (A) would become   (C) won't become
   (B) became   (D) wouldn't have become

   A B C D

8. I'm going to Gerry's for Thanksgiving, but I can't stand to eat turkey. What _____ if that happened to you?
   (A) would you do   (C) do you do
   (B) did you do   (D) will you do

   A B C D

9. If I _____ you, I'd just go for dessert.
   (A) am   (C) were
   (B) was   (D) had been

   A B C D

10. I'm so busy these days. I wish I _____ more free time.
    (A) had   (C) have
    (B) had had   (D) would have

    A B C D

(continued on next page)

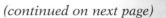

359

11. What _____ if you didn't have to work for six months?　　　A　B　C　D
(A) would you do　　　　(C) did you do
(B) will you do　　　　　(D) have you done

12. If I were free for six months, I _____ around the world.　　　A　B　C　D
(A) traveled　　　　(C) travel
(B) 'd travel　　　　(D) 'll travel

13. It's very hot. If you drink some water, you _____ better.　　　A　B　C　D
(A) feel　　　　(C) have felt
(B) felt　　　　(D) might feel

14. I _____ nervous whenever I fly.　　　A　B　C　D
(A) would get　　　　(C) 'll get
(B) get　　　　　　　(D) had gotten

15. Unless they _____ ticket prices, I'm not going to fly anymore.　　　A　B　C　D
(A) don't lower　　　　(C) would lower
(B) lowered　　　　　　(D) lower

16. Your roommate is really noisy. If I _____ with him, I'd talk to him about the problem.　　　A　B　C　D
(A) lived　　　　(C) live
(B) 'll live　　　　(D) would live

17. If he _____ soon, I'll probably move.　　　A　B　C　D
(A) doesn't change　　　　(C) wouldn't change
(B) wouldn't　　　　　　　(D) didn't change

18. What would you have done if you _____ the lottery last week?　　　A　B　C　D
(A) win　　　　(C) 'd have won
(B) 'd won　　　(D) 'll win

19. Whenever there's a thunderstorm, the cat _____ under the bed.　　　A　B　C　D
(A) is hiding　　　　(C) hides
(B) would hide　　　(D) hid

20. I didn't like Florida. I wish we _____ to vacation there.　　　A　B　C　D
(A) haven't decided　　　　(C) didn't decide
(B) hadn't decided　　　　 (D) won't decide

21. Mary _____ the exam unless she had hired a tutor.　　　A　B　C　D
(A) couldn't have passed　　(C) couldn't pass
(B) can't pass　　　　　　　(D) could pass

22. When Carlos has a headache, he _____ some tea.　　　A　B　C　D
(A) would drink　　　　(C) 's drunk
(B) drank　　　　　　　(D) drinks

23. If Sami doesn't call soon, we _____ without him.　　　A　B　C　D
(A) 're going to leave　　　(C) 'd leave
(B) left　　　　　　　　　　(D) 'd have left

II. *Complete the conversation with the correct form of the verbs in parentheses.*

A: Where were you Sunday night?

B: Home. I had to study for Spanish.

A: If you _____had come_____ with us, you _____ an awesome movie.
   1. (come)   2. (see)

B: Yeah? What?

A: *Back to the Future.* It's about a kid who time-travels back to his parents' high-school

   days. He changes his own future. It's so cool. At the end, his parents . . .

B: Wait—don't tell me. If you _____ me the ending, you
                                    3. (tell)

   _____ it for me. I want to see it myself.
        4. (spoil)

A: OK. But have you ever thought about that?

B: About what?

A: About how things could be different. You grew up here in Baileyville, and

   you're almost an adult now. But what _____ your childhood

   _____ like if you _____ in a different family?
        5. (be)   6. (be born)

B: Let's see. If I _____ a different family, I _____ here
                        7. (have)   8. (not grow up)

   in Baileyville.

A: Right. And if you _____ here, I _____ you.
                        9. (not grow up)   10. (not meet)

B: That's true. But getting back to the here-and-now, how did you do on the Spanish test?

A: I flunked. I wish I _____ that course. I'm afraid I'm going to fail.
                        11. (not take)

B: You just don't study enough. If you _____ more, you
                                            12. (study)

   _____ this course easily this semester.
        13. (pass)

A: That's easy for you to say. You always get A's.

B: Sometimes I don't. It's not automatic. I _____ A's unless I
                                                14. (not get)

   _____.
        15. (study)

A: I suppose you're right.

B: If I _____ you, I _____ to get better grades. It's
            16. (be)   17. (try)

   important for your future.

III. *Complete the news article with the correct form of the verbs in parentheses. Choose the affirmative or the negative form of the verb.*

What Would You Do? BY DEWITT RITE

Imagine that you are unemployed and have a family to support. What ___would___

you _____do_____ if you _____ a wallet in the street?
      1. (do)   **2. (find)**

_____ you _____ the money if you _____
      3. (keep)   **4. (know)**

no one would ever find out?

    When Lara Williams faced that situation last week, she brought the wallet to the police,

who traced it to Mr. and Mrs. Asuki, tourists from Japan. The Asukis were pleasantly

surprised to see the wallet—and their money—again. "If we _____ the
                 5. (get)

money back, we _____ money for the rest of our trip. It
      6. (borrow)

_____ a long time to pay back that debt," beamed Mrs. Asuki.
      7. (take)

    The police officer who handled the situation was not surprised, however. "Most people

are honest," commented Lieutenant Kronsky. "If they _____, our job
                 8. (be)

_____ even harder than it is."
      9. (be)

    Did Mrs. Williams have a hard time making her decision? "Frankly, yes. We need

the money. I _____ Mr. Asuki's wallet in the gutter unless I
      10. (see)

_____ down just at that moment. For a little while, it seemed like fate
      11. (glance)

had sent it to us. But whenever I _____ a difficult decision to make,
                 12. (have)

I always _____ the problem with my husband. We both knew what was
      13. (discuss)

right in this situation. We always tell our kids, if something _____ to
                 14. (belong)

you, _____ it. Our kids _____ the rules unless we
      15. (return)   **16. (follow)**

_____ the rules ourselves."
      17. (obey)

    The Asukis have offered the Williamses a reward, and a friendship has sprung up

between the two families. "If the Williams family ever _____ to Japan,
                 18. (come)

they _____ our guests," said Mr. and Mrs. Asuki.
      19. (be)

IV. *Rewrite each sentence or group of sentences as a wish.*

1. I want spring vacation to last six months.

    I wish spring vacation lasted six months.

2. I didn't buy business-class tickets. I'm sorry I didn't.

_____

3. Oh, no. The in-flight movie is *Back to the Future II*. I hate that one.

_____

4. I'm sorry that we went to Disneyland on vacation.

_____

5. The beach is a better place to go.

_____

6. Florida's nice. I'd like to live there.

_____

7. Maybe my office can transfer me to Orlando.

_____

V. *Each sentence has four underlined words or phrases. The four underlined parts of the sentences are marked A, B, C, or D. Circle the letter of the <u>one</u> underlined word or phrase that is NOT CORRECT.*

1. <u>Whenever</u> we <u>will get</u> a long <u>holiday,</u> my family <u>takes</u> a trip.   A Ⓑ C D
    A   B   C   D

2. We <u>always</u> <u>went</u> camping <u>if</u> we don't <u>get</u> a lot of time off.   A B C D
    A   B   C   D

3. <u>Unless</u> we <u>had</u> <u>gone</u> to Florida last year, I wouldn't <u>had known</u> how   A B C D
    A   B   C   D
great Disneyland was.

4. If I <u>am</u> older, I <u>would</u> <u>try</u> <u>to get</u> a job in Florida.   A B C D
      A   B   C   D

5. We <u>could</u> <u>had</u> seen <u>more</u> if the lines <u>had been</u> shorter.   A B C D
    A   B   C   D

6. I <u>wish</u> my friend <u>could have</u> <u>came</u> with us when we <u>went</u> last year.   A B C D
    A   B   C   D

7. <u>Unless</u> you're interested in the movies, you <u>can</u> <u>visit</u> Universal   A B C D
    A   B   C
Studios and <u>see</u> all the movie sets.
           D

8. <u>If</u> you stay a <u>week</u>, you <u>would</u> <u>have</u> more time to do things.   A B C D
    A   B   C   D

▶ *To check your answers, go to the Answer Key on page 366.*

FROM GRAMMAR TO WRITING SHOWING CAUSE AND EFFECT

One way to develop a topic is to discuss its causes and effects. To show cause and effect you can connect **sentences** with *as a result* and *therefore*. In individual sentences, you can connect **clauses** with *so, because,* or *if.*

EXAMPLE:

CAUSE	EFFECT
I was shy.	*I didn't talk in class.* ⟶

I was shy. **As a result,** I didn't talk in class.

I was shy. **Therefore,** I didn't talk in class.

I was shy, **so** I didn't talk in class.

Because I was shy, I didn't talk in class.

If I hadn't been shy, I would have talked in class.

PUNCTUATION NOTE
Use a comma <u>after</u> *as a result* and *therefore.* Use a comma <u>before</u> *so.* Use a comma <u>after</u> a clause beginning with *because* or *if* when it comes before the main clause.

---

1 *Read the essay. Underline once sentences or clauses that show a cause. Underline twice sentences or clauses that show an effect. Circle the connecting words.*

My biggest problem in school is my fear of talking in class. My hands always shake if I answer a question or present a paper. If it is a big assignment, I even feel sick to my stomach.

There are several causes for my problem, but my family's attitude is the most important. My family motto is, "Children should be seen, but not heard." Because my parents never ask for our opinions, we never give them. I can feel my mother's disapproval if a talkative friend visits. In addition, my parents classify their children. My older brother is the "Smart One." I am the "Creative One." I think I would do better in school if they expected more, but they don't expect much. Therefore, I have not tried very hard.

Recently I decided to do something about my problem. I discovered that I feel less nervous about giving a speech in class if I role-play my presentation with a friend. I have also joined a discussion club. As a result, I get a lot of practice talking. My problem has causes, so it must have solutions!

2 *Connect the following sentences. Use the word in parentheses.*

a. Mr. Stewart didn't help me. I never spoke in class. (if)

If Mr. Stewart hadn't helped me, I never would have spoken in class.

b. He believed in me. I became more courageous. (because)

_____

c. We worked in groups. I got used to talking about ideas with classmates. (so)

_____

d. I have gotten a lot of practice. I feel more confident. (as a result)

_____

e. Sena didn't understand the question. She didn't raise her hand. (therefore)

_____

3 *Before you write . . .*

• Work with a partner. Discuss the causes of a strong feeling that you have.

• Complete this outline for a cause and effect essay.

PARAGRAPH I The feeling you are going to write about: _____

One or two examples: _____

PARAGRAPH II The causes and effects of the feeling:

A. _____

B. _____

C. _____

PARAGRAPH III How you deal with the feeling:

A. _____

B. _____

4 *Write a three-paragraph essay about the causes and effects of a feeling that you have. Use your outline to organize your writing.*

5 *Exchange your essay with a different partner. Outline your partner's essay. Write questions about things that are not clear.*

6 *Discuss the essay with your partner. Then rewrite your own essay.*

REVIEW OR SELFTEST
ANSWER KEY

I. (Units 21–24)

2.	A	13.	D
3.	B	14.	B
4.	C	15.	D
5.	B	16.	A
6.	C	17.	A
7.	D	18.	B
8.	A	19.	C
9.	C	20.	B
10.	A	21.	A
11.	A	22.	D
12.	B	23.	A

II. (Units 21–24)

2. would have seen
3. tell
4. 'll spoil
5. would . . . have been
6. 'd been born
7. 'd had
8. wouldn't have grown up
9. hadn't grown up
10. wouldn't have met
11. hadn't taken
12. studied OR study
13. 'd pass OR 'll pass
14. don't get OR wouldn't get
15. study OR studied
16. were
17. 'd try

III. (Units 21–24)

2. found
3. Would . . . keep
4. knew
5. hadn't gotten
6. would've borrowed
7. would've taken
8. weren't
9. would be
10. wouldn't have seen
11. had glanced
12. have
13. discuss
14. doesn't belong
15. return
16. won't follow
17. obey
18. comes
19. 'll be

IV. (Units 23–24)

2. I wish I had bought business-class tickets.
3. I wish the in-flight movie weren't *Back to the Future II.*
4. I wish we hadn't gone to Disneyland on vacation.
5. I wish we had gone to the beach.
6. I wish I OR we lived in Florida.
7. I wish my office could transfer me to Orlando.

V. (Units 21–24)

2.	B	6.	C
3.	D	7.	A
4.	A	8.	C
5.	B		

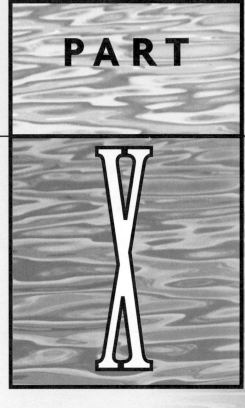

PART

X

INDIRECT SPEECH AND EMBEDDED QUESTIONS

25 DIRECT AND INDIRECT SPEECH

GRAMMAR **IN CONTEXT**

BEFORE YOU READ Explain the cartoon. Is it ever all right to tell a lie? If so, in what situations?

Read this magazine article about lying.

THE TRUTH ABOUT LYING

BY JENNIFER MORALES

At 9:00 Rick Spivak's bank telephoned and **said his credit card payment was late**. "**The check is in the mail**," Rick replied quickly. At 11:45 Rick left for a 12:00 meeting across town. Arriving late, Rick **told his client that traffic had been bad**. That evening, Rick's fiancée wore a new dress. Rick hated it. "**It looks just great on you**," he said.

Three lies in one day! Yet Rick is just an ordinary guy. Each time, he **told himself that sometimes the truth causes too many problems**. Most of us tell white lies, harmless untruths that help us avoid trouble. These are our four most frequent reasons:

◆ To get something more quickly or to avoid unpleasant situations: "**I have to have that report by 5:00 today**," or "**I tried to call you, but your line was busy**."

◆ To appear more acceptable to a new friend or to feel better about yourself: "**I run a mile every day**," or "**I'm looking better these days**."

◆ To make a polite excuse: "**I'd love to go to your party, but I have to work**."

◆ To protect someone else's feelings: "**That tie looks great on you**."

Is telling lies a new trend? The majority of people in a recent survey **said that people were more honest ten years ago**. Nevertheless, lying wasn't really born yesterday. In the eighteenth century, the French philosopher Vauvenargues told the truth about lying when he wrote, "**All men are born truthful and die liars**."

It looks just great on you.

GRAMMAR **PRESENTATION**
DIRECT AND INDIRECT SPEECH

DIRECT SPEECH		
DIRECT STATEMENT	**SUBJECT**	**REPORTING VERB**
"The check **is** in the mail," "The dress **looks** good on you," "The traffic **was** bad,"	he	**said.**

DIRECT SPEECH		
SUBJECT	**REPORTING VERB**	**DIRECT STATEMENT**
He	**said,**	"The check **is** in the mail." "The dress **looks** good on you." "The traffic **was** bad."

INDIRECT SPEECH				
SUBJECT	**REPORTING VERB**	**NOUN / PRONOUN**	**INDIRECT STATEMENT**	
He	**told**	his client Ann her	**(that)**	the check **was** in the mail. the dress **looked** good on her. the traffic **had been** bad.
	said			

NOTES	EXAMPLES

1. Speech may be reported in two ways:

a. Direct speech (also called quoted speech) states <u>the exact words</u> that a speaker used. In writing, put <u>quotation marks</u> before and after the speech you are quoting.

(See Appendix 22 on page A-9 for the punctuation rules for direct speech.)

- **"The check is in the mail,"** he said.
- **"I like that tie,"** she told him.
  OR
- He said, **"The check is in the mail."**
- She told him, **"I like that tie."**

b. Indirect speech (also called reported speech) reports what a speaker said <u>without using the exact words</u>. The word ***that*** can introduce indirect speech.

- He said **the check was in the mail**.
- She told him **that she liked that tie**.

▶ **BE CAREFUL!** Do not use quotation marks when writing indirect speech.

- She said **she had to work**.
  NOT ~~She said "she had to work."~~

---

2. The **reporting verb** (such as ***say*** or ***tell***) is usually in the **simple past tense** for both direct and indirect speech.

DIRECT SPEECH
- "It's a great dress," he **said**.

INDIRECT SPEECH
- He **told** her that it was a great dress.

USAGE NOTE: When you <u>mention the listener</u>, it is preferable to use the verb ***tell*** as the reporting verb in both direct and indirect speech.

However, the verb ***say*** can also be used in these cases.

- "I'm sorry to be late," Rick **told Ann**.
- Rick **told her** he was sorry to be late.
  OR
- "I'm sorry to be late," Rick **said to Ann**.
- Rick **said to her** he was sorry to be late.

▶ **BE CAREFUL!** Do not use the verb ***tell*** when the <u>listener is not mentioned</u>.

- He **said** he had been sick.
  NOT ~~He told he had been sick.~~

---

3. When the reporting verb is in the simple past tense, the **verb in the indirect speech statement** is often in a <u>different tense</u> from the verb in the direct speech statement.

In direct speech if the speaker made a statement using the <u>simple present tense</u>, the indirect speech statement often uses the <u>simple past tense</u>.

DIRECT SPEECH
- "I ***buy*** shoes on sale," she **said**.

INDIRECT SPEECH
- She **said** she ***bought*** shoes on sale.

If in direct speech the speaker made a statement in the <u>simple past tense</u>, the indirect speech statement often uses the <u>past perfect</u>.

(See Unit 26 for additional tense changes in indirect speech.)

Direct Speech
- "I *found* a great store," she **said**.

Indirect Speech
- She **said** she *had found* a great store.

---

4. In indirect speech the **verb tense change is optional** when reporting:

a. something someone has **just said**.

A: I'm tired from all that shopping.
B: What did you say?
A: I **said** I*'m* tired. OR I **said** I *was* tired.

b. something that is **still true**.

- Rick **said** the bank *wants* a check.
  OR
- Rick **said** the bank *wanted* a check.

c. a **general truth** or **scientific law**.

- Mrs. Smith **told** her students that water *freezes* at 0° Celsius.
  OR
- Mrs. Smith **told** her students that water *froze* at 0° Celsius.

---

5. When the **reporting verb** is in the **present tense**, <u>do not change the verb tense</u> in indirect speech.

Note that in newspapers, reporting verbs are often in the present tense.

(See Appendix 13 on page A-5 for a list of verbs used to report speech.)

- She **says** that she *runs* a mile every day.

- Fifty-seven percent of women **report** that they always *tell* the truth.

---

6. In **indirect speech**, make changes in **pronouns and possessives** to <u>keep the speaker's original meaning</u>.

- Rick told Ann, "**I** like **your** dress."

- Rick told Ann that *he* liked *her* dress.

FOCUSED PRACTICE

1 DISCOVER THE GRAMMAR

Read this magazine article. Circle the reporting verbs. Underline once all the examples of direct speech. Underline twice all the examples of indirect speech.

Lying on the Job

"Lying during a job interview is risky business," (says) Martha Toledo, director of the management consulting firm Maxwell. "The truth has a funny way of coming out." Toledo tells the story of one woman applying for a job as an office manager. The woman told the interviewer that she had a B.A. degree. Actually, she was eight credits short. She also said that she had made $30,000 at her last job. The truth was $5,000 less. "Many firms really do check facts," warns Toledo. In this case, a call to the applicant's company revealed the discrepancies.

Toledo relates a story about another job applicant, Gloria. During an interview, Gloria reported that she had quit her last job. Gloria landed the new job and was doing well until the company hired another employee, Pete. Gloria and Pete had worked at the same company. Pete eventually told his boss that his old company had fired Gloria.

2 CONFESSIONS   Grammar Notes 2, 5, 6

Complete this student's essay with the correct words.

Once when I was a teenager, I went to my Aunt Leah's house. Aunt Leah collected

pottery, and as soon as I got there, she _____*told*_____ me she _____ to
                                        1. (said / told)   2. (wants / wanted)

show me _____ new bowl. She _____ she _____
          3. (my / her)   4. (said / told)   5. (has / had)

just bought it. It was beautiful, and after I heard the price, I knew why. When Aunt Leah went

to answer the door, I picked up the bowl. It slipped from my hands and smashed to pieces

on the floor. As Aunt Leah walked back into the room, I screamed and _____
                                                                       6. (said / told)

that the cat had just broken _____ new bowl. Aunt Leah got this funny look
                              7. (her / your)

on her face and _____ me that it _____ important.
                  8. (said / told)   9. (isn't / wasn't)

I didn't sleep at all that night, and the next morning, I called my aunt and

_____ her that I had broken _____ bowl. She said
10. (said / told)   11. (her / your)

_____'d known that all along. We still laugh about the story today.
12. (I / she)

3 TO BE HONEST

*Look at the pictures. Rewrite the statements as indirect speech. Use **said** as the reporting verb and make necessary changes in verbs and pronouns.*

1.

She said it was her own recipe.

2.

_____

_____

3.

_____

_____

4.

_____

_____

5.

_____

_____

6.

_____

_____

4 THEN SHE SAID

Report the conversation between Ben and Lisa. Use the reporting verbs in parentheses. Make necessary changes in verbs and pronouns.

1. LISA: I just heard about a job at a scientific research company.

(tell) _She told him she had just heard about a job at scientific research company._

2. BEN: Oh, I majored in science at Florida State.

(say) _He said that he had majored in science at Florida State._

3. LISA: The starting salary is good.

(say) _____

4. BEN: I need more money.

(say) _____

5. LISA: They want someone with some experience as a programmer.

(say) _____

6. BEN: Well, I work as a programmer for Data Systems.

(tell) _____

7. LISA: Oh—they need a college graduate.

(say) _____

8. BEN: Well, I graduated from Florida State.

(tell) _____

9. LISA: But they don't want a recent graduate.

(say) _____

10. BEN: I got my degree four years ago.

(tell) _____

11. LISA: It sounds like the right job for you.

(tell) _____

12. BEN: I think so too.

(say) _____

COMMUNICATION PRACTICE

5 LISTENING

Read Lisa's weekly planner. Then listen to the conversations. Lisa wasn't always honest. Listen again and note the differences between what Lisa said and the truth.

SATURDAY		MONDAY
Morning		Morning
Afternoon		Afternoon
Evening	*6:00 date with Ben!*	*6:00 vegetarian cooking class* Evening
		7:30 dinner with Chris
SUNDAY	*sleep late!*	TUESDAY
Morning	*9:00 ~~aerobics class~~*	Morning
Afternoon		*4:00 weekly staff meeting — present sales report* Afternoon
Evening		Evening

Now write sentences about Lisa's white lies.

1. She said her parents were in town, but she has a date with Ben.

2. _____

3. _____

4. _____

6 WHY LIE?

Review the four types of lies described in The Truth About Lying *on page 368. Work in small groups. Is it OK to lie in these four circumstances? Give examples from your own experience to support your ideas.*

EXAMPLE:
Once my friend told me that my haircut looked great, but it really looked awful. I think she should have told me the truth. Now it's hard for me to believe anything she says.

7 HONESTY QUESTIONNAIRE

Complete the questionnaire about yourself. Then work in groups. Report your group's results to the rest of the class.

	Always	Usually	Sometimes	Rarely	Never
1. I tell the truth to friends.					
2. I tell the truth to my family.					
3. It's OK to lie on the job.					
4. "White lies" protect people's feelings.					
5. Most people are honest.					
6. It's best to tell the truth.					
7. I tell people my real age.					
8. My friends are honest with me.					
9. It's difficult to tell a convincing lie.					
10. Politicians are honest.					
11. Doctors tell their patients the whole truth.					
12. I answer questionnaires honestly.					

EXAMPLE:
Five of us said that we usually told the truth.
Only one of us said it was always best to tell the truth.

8 TO TELL THE TRUTH

Play this game with the whole class. Three "contestants" leave the room. They choose one experience to report to the class. Only one contestant has actually had the experience. The other two must tell convincing lies to make the class believe that they are the ones who have had the experience.

After the contestants choose the experience they will relate, they go back into the room and sit in front of the class. Each contestant states the experience. Then class members ask each contestant detailed questions about it.

EXAMPLE:
CONTESTANT A: Once I climbed a 10,000-meter-high mountain.
CONTESTANT B: Once I climbed a 10,000-meter-high mountain.
CONTESTANT C: Once I climbed a 10,000-meter-high mountain.
CLASS MEMBER: Contestant A, how long did it take you?
Contestant B, how long did it take *you*?
Contestant C, how many people were with you?

After each contestant has answered questions, decide which contestant is telling the truth. Explain which statements convinced you that someone was lying or telling the truth.

EXAMPLE:

I believed Contestant A because she said that it had taken her two days.

I think C was lying. He said he'd climbed the mountain alone.

9 QUOTABLE QUOTES

In groups, discuss these famous quotations about lying. Do you agree with them? Give examples to support your opinion. Use **says** *to report the proverbs and* **said** *to report the ideas of individuals.*

All men are born truthful and die liars.
   —*Vauvenargues (French philosopher, 1715–1747)*

EXAMPLE:

Vauvenargues said that all men are born truthful and die liars.

I agree because babies don't lie, but children and adults do.

A half truth is a whole lie.
   —*Jewish proverb*

A little inaccuracy saves tons of explanation.
   —*Saki (British short-story writer, 1870–1916)*

A liar needs a good memory.
   —*Quintilian (First-century Roman orator)*

The man who speaks the truth is always at ease.
   —*Persian proverb*

The cruelest lies are often told in silence.
   —*Robert Louis Stevenson (Scottish novelist, 1850–1894)*

10 WRITING

Read the conversation between Rick and Ann. Then write a paragraph reporting what they said.

RICK: Hi, honey. Sorry I'm late.

ANN: That's all right. I made liver and onions. It's almost ready.

RICK: *(looking upset)* It smells great, honey. It's one of my favorites.

ANN: You look upset!

RICK: I'm OK. I had a rough day at work. Oh, I stopped and bought some frogs' legs for dinner on Wednesday. It's my turn to cook.

ANN: *(looking upset)* That's interesting. I look forward to trying them.

EXAMPLE:

Rick came home and said he was sorry he was late. Ann said that was all right.

26 INDIRECT SPEECH: TENSE CHANGES

GRAMMAR **IN CONTEXT**

BEFORE YOU READ   Look at the pictures. What is happening? What do you think the title of the article means?

Read this excerpt from a news magazine article.

By **Kenji Yamaguchi**

In late August 1992, meteorologists from the National Hurricane Center in Florida noticed a small tropical storm over West Africa. When the storm grew stronger and moved west, they named it Andrew. A few days after that, Lixion Avila of the National Hurricane Center, who had been tracking Andrew all night, called his boss at 3:00 A.M. and told him **that they had a hurricane**. Andrew quickly grew into a force four, and the National Hurricane Center went on the air to warn Florida residents **that a giant storm was coming**. They said **Andrew might even become a force five**–the most powerful class of hurricanes.

Government workers told people **that they had to leave homes near the coast**, and television reporters announced **that everyone should buy extra food and water**. As Floridians prepared for Hurricane Andrew, stores and gas stations reported **that they could not keep up with demands for canned food, bottled water, and gasoline**.

(continued on next page)

In spite of their preparation, Andrew's 170-mile-an-hour winds caused terrible damage. After the storm, officials at the National Hurricane Center reported **that the electricity had gone out and the radar had been torn off the roof of the twelve-story center**.

Those in private homes suffered most. One family said **they had run from room to room with windows exploding all around them**. Jim Jenkins, who had just moved to Florida in June, told a reporter **that if he had known what a force-four hurricane was like, he would have left immediately**. He said **that he and his family had spent a terrifying night in a closet after a trailer had blown through the house**. Jim said, "There are no words to describe this storm."

After the terror came the realization of loss. In one trailer park, a young woman held her baby as she sifted through the scraps of metal that had been their home. Her husband, still dazed, told us **that he had lost his home, his job, and his dog in just two hours**. While the government struggled to provide emergency

services for the victims, officials predicted **it would cost at least $20 billion to rebuild after Andrew**.

Naming Hurricanes

- Hurricanes receive names (like *Andrew*) to avoid confusion when more than one storm is being observed.
- Hurricanes are named by the World Meteorological Organization.
- When a storm results in a large loss of life or property damage, its name is "retired." (*Andrew* was retired and replaced by *Alex*.)
- Before 1979, hurricanes were only given women's names.
- Today hurricanes alternate between men's and women's names in alphabetical order (*Alex, Bonnie, Charley, Danielle*, etc.).
- There are no hurricanes that begin with the letters Q, U, X, Y, or Z.

GRAMMAR **PRESENTATION**
INDIRECT SPEECH: TENSE CHANGES

DIRECT SPEECH			INDIRECT SPEECH				
SUBJECT	**REPORTING VERB**	**DIRECT STATEMENT**	**SUBJECT**	**REPORTING VERB**	**NOUN / PRONOUN**		**INDIRECT STATEMENT**
He	said,	"I **live** in Miami."	He	told	Jim	(that)	he **lived** in Miami.
		"I **moved** here in June."			me		he **had moved** there in June.
		"I**'m looking** for an apartment."			you		he **was looking** for an apartment.
		"I**'ve started** a new job."			him		he **had started** a new job.
		"I**'m going to stay** here."			her		he **was going to stay** there.
		"I**'ll invite** you for the holidays."			us		he **would invite** me for the holidays.
		"We **can go** swimming."			them		we **could go** swimming.
		"I **may look** for a roommate."					he **might look** for a roommate.
		"I **should get** back to work."					he **should get** back to work.
		"I **have to finish** my report."		said			he **had to finish** his report.
		"You **must come** to visit."					I/we **had to come** to visit.
		"We **ought to see** each other more often."					we **ought to see** each other more often.

NOTES	**EXAMPLES**

1. As you learned in Unit 25, when the <u>reporting verb is in the simple past tense</u>, the **verb tense in the indirect speech statement often changes.**

DIRECT SPEECH		INDIRECT SPEECH
Simple present	→	Simple past
Present progressive	→	Past progressive
Simple past tense	→	Past perfect
Present perfect	→	Past perfect

DIRECT SPEECH	INDIRECT SPEECH
He said, "It**'s** windy."	He said it **was** windy.
She said, "A storm **is coming**."	She said a storm **was coming**.
He said, "Tom **called**."	He said Tom **had called**.
She told him, "I**'ve heard** the news."	She told him that she **had heard** the news.

2. Modals often change in indirect speech.

DIRECT SPEECH		INDIRECT SPEECH
will	→	*would*
can	→	*could*
may	→	*might*
must	→	*had to*

DIRECT SPEECH	INDIRECT SPEECH
I said, "The winds **will be** strong."	I said the winds **would be** strong.
"You **can stay** with us," they told us.	They told us we **could stay** with them.
He said, "The storm **may last** all night."	He said that the storm **might last** all night.
"You **must leave**," he told us.	He told us we **had to leave**.

3. Some verbs do not change in indirect speech.

a. Do not change *should*, *could*, *might*, and *ought to* in indirect speech.

DIRECT SPEECH	INDIRECT SPEECH
"You **should listen** to the weather report," he told us.	He told us that we **should listen** to the weather report.
"You **ought to buy** water," he said.	He said we **ought to buy** water.

(continued on next page)

	DIRECT SPEECH	INDIRECT SPEECH
b. Do not change the <u>past perfect</u> in indirect speech.	"I **had** just **moved** here a week before," she said.	She said she **had** just **moved** here a week before.
c. Do not change verbs in <u>present and past unreal conditional</u> sentences in indirect speech.	"If I **knew**, I **would tell** you," said Jim.	Jim said if he **knew**, he **would tell** me.
	"If I **had known**, I **would have told** you," said Jim.	He said if he **had known** he **would have told** me.
d. Do not change <u>past modals</u> in indirect speech.	"I **should have left**."	He said that he **should have left**.
	"We **couldn't have known**."	They said that they **couldn't have known**.

---

4. Change time phrases in indirect speech to keep the speaker's original meaning.

DIRECT SPEECH		INDIRECT SPEECH
now	→	**then**
today	→	**tomorrow**
tomorrow	→	**the next day**
yesterday	→	**the day before**
this week / month / year	→	**that week / month / year**
last week / month / year	→	**the week / month / year before**
next week / month / year	→	**the following week / month / year**

Sam to Kate:
• I just got home **yesterday**. I'll start cleaning up **tomorrow**.

Kate to Rick (a few days later):
• Sam told me he had just gotten home **the day before**. He said he would start cleaning up **the next day**.

Lulu to her mother (right after the storm):
• Our home won't be repaired until **next month**.

The family newsletter (two months later):
• Lulu reported that their home wouldn't be repaired until **the following month**.

---

5. Change *here* and *this* in indirect speech to keep the speaker's original meaning.

DIRECT SPEECH		INDIRECT SPEECH
here	→	**there**
this	→	**that**

Jim (in Florida) to Erica (in New Jersey):
• I love it **here**. **This** climate is great.

Erica to Susan (both in New Jersey):
• Jim said he loved it **there**. He told me **that** that climate was great.

FOCUSED PRACTICE

1 DISCOVER THE GRAMMAR

Read the indirect speech. Then circle the letter of the direct speech that is being reported.

1. The local weather forecaster said that it was going to be a terrible storm.

   a. "It was going to be a terrible storm."

   b. "It's going to be a terrible storm."

   c. "It was a terrible storm."

2. She said the winds might reach 170 miles per hour.

   a. "The winds reached 170 miles per hour."

   b. "The winds would reach 170 miles per hour."

   c. "The winds may reach 170 miles per hour."

3. She said there would be more rain the next day.

   a. "There will be more rain the next day."

   b. "There would be more rain tomorrow."

   c. "There will be more rain tomorrow."

4. She told people that they should try to leave the area.

   a. "You should try to leave the area."

   b. "You should have tried to leave the area."

   c. "You would leave the area."

5. She reported that people were leaving the coastal towns.

   a. "People are leaving the coastal towns."

   b. "People were leaving the coastal towns."

   c. "People left the coastal towns."

6. She said that they could expect a lot of damage.

   a. "We could expect a lot of damage."

   b. "We could have expected a lot of damage."

   c. "We can expect a lot of damage."

7. She said that Andrew was the worst hurricane they had had there.

   a. "Andrew is the worst hurricane we have here."

   b. "Andrew is the worst hurricane we have had here."

   c. "Andrew is the worst hurricane we have had there."

8. She told them that the Red Cross had arrived the day before.

   a. "The Red Cross arrived the day before."

   b. "The Red Cross arrived yesterday."

   c. "The Red Cross arrived today."

(continued on next page)

9. She reported that the president would be there to inspect the damage.

    a. "The president will be here to inspect the damage."

    b. "The president will be there to inspect the damage."

    c. "The president would be there to inspect the damage."

10. She said that if they hadn't had time to prepare, the danger would have been even greater.

    a. "If we hadn't had time to prepare, the danger would have been even greater."

    b. "If we don't have time to prepare, the danger will be even greater."

    c. "If we didn't have time to prepare, the danger would be even greater."

2 RUMORS

Grammar Notes 1–5

You are in Florida. Imagine you heard these rumors yesterday, and you are reporting them today. Use **They said** *to report the rumors.*

1. "The hurricane changed direction last night."

    They said that the hurricane had changed direction the night before.

2. "It's going to pass north of here."

3. "The Texaco station ran out of gas this afternoon."

4. "It's not really a hurricane, just a tropical storm."

5. "They've closed the bridge because of high tides."

6. "They won't restore the electricity until tomorrow."

7. "They can't reopen the schools for at least a week."

8. "You ought to use bottled water for a few days."

3 **HURRICANE**

Read this interview between radio station WFLA and meteorologist Ronald Myers.

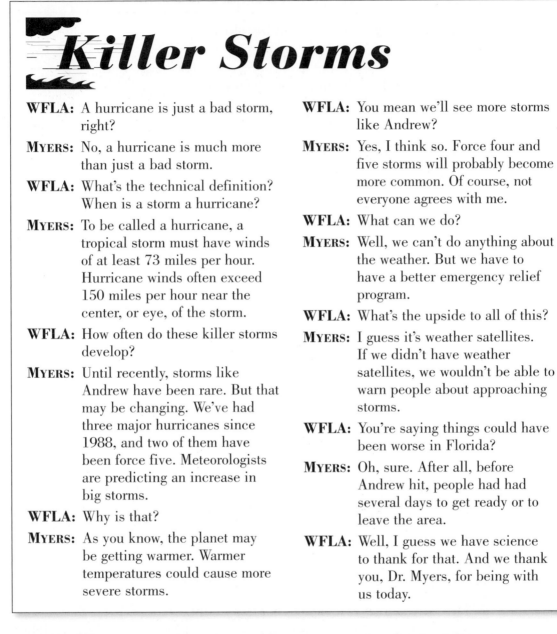

Killer Storms

WFLA: A hurricane is just a bad storm, right?

MYERS: No, a hurricane is much more than just a bad storm.

WFLA: What's the technical definition? When is a storm a hurricane?

MYERS: To be called a hurricane, a tropical storm must have winds of at least 73 miles per hour. Hurricane winds often exceed 150 miles per hour near the center, or eye, of the storm.

WFLA: How often do these killer storms develop?

MYERS: Until recently, storms like Andrew have been rare. But that may be changing. We've had three major hurricanes since 1988, and two of them have been force five. Meteorologists are predicting an increase in big storms.

WFLA: Why is that?

MYERS: As you know, the planet may be getting warmer. Warmer temperatures could cause more severe storms.

WFLA: You mean we'll see more storms like Andrew?

MYERS: Yes, I think so. Force four and five storms will probably become more common. Of course, not everyone agrees with me.

WFLA: What can we do?

MYERS: Well, we can't do anything about the weather. But we have to have a better emergency relief program.

WFLA: What's the upside to all of this?

MYERS: I guess it's weather satellites. If we didn't have weather satellites, we wouldn't be able to warn people about approaching storms.

WFLA: You're saying things could have been worse in Florida?

MYERS: Oh, sure. After all, before Andrew hit, people had had several days to get ready or to leave the area.

WFLA: Well, I guess we have science to thank for that. And we thank you, Dr. Myers, for being with us today.

*Now read the following statements. For each statement write **That's right** or **That's wrong** and report what Dr. Myers said.*

1. A hurricane is just a bad storm.

   That's wrong. He said a hurricane was much more than just a bad storm.

2. Hurricane winds often exceed 150 miles per hour.

(continued on next page)

3. Until recently, force-five hurricanes have been rare.

_____

4. We've had two major hurricanes since 1988.

_____

5. Meteorologists are predicting an increase in big storms.

_____

6. Warmer temperatures could cause more severe storms.

_____

7. Force-five storms will probably become more common.

_____

8. We can do something about the weather.

_____

9. We have to have a better emergency relief program.

_____

10. If we didn't have weather satellites, we wouldn't be able to warn people.

_____

11. Things could have been worse in Florida.

_____

12. Before Andrew hit, people in Florida had had no time to leave the area.

_____

4 WEATHER REPORTS   Grammar Notes 1–5

Jim and Rita live in Florida. Read the information that Jim got during the day.
Then write what people said. Use direct speech.

Jim's mother told him that she was listening to the weather report. She said that she was worried about Jim and Rita. She told him that if they weren't so stubborn they'd pack up and leave right then.

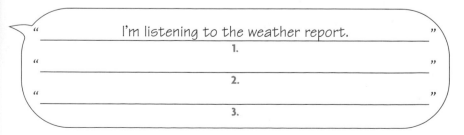

" I'm listening to the weather report. "
_____
1.

" _____ "
2.

" _____ "
3.

Jim's father gave him some good advice. He said he'd had a lot of experience with hurricanes. He said Jim and Rita had to put tape on all their windows. He also told Jim that they ought to fill the sinks and bathtubs with water. He said they should buy a lot of batteries.

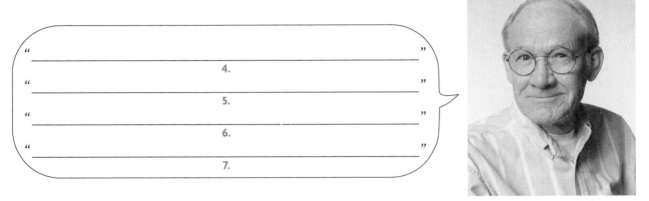

" _____ "
4.
" _____ "
5.
" _____ "
6.
" _____ "
7.

Sue called. She and Sara are worried. Their place is too close to the coast. They said that they couldn't stay there, and they told Jim that they wanted to stay with him and Rita. They said they were leaving that night. They told Jim they should have called him and Rita sooner.

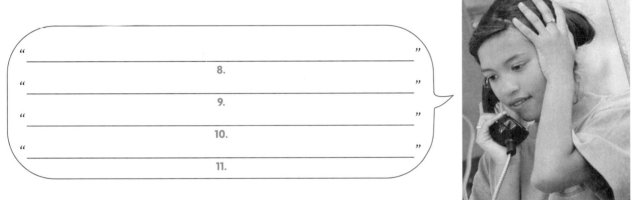

" _____ "
8.
" _____ "
9.
" _____ "
10.
" _____ "
11.

Jim listened to the weather advisory in the afternoon. The forecaster said the storm would hit the coast that night. She warned that the eye of the hurricane was going to pass over that area, and she said that the storm might last for several hours.

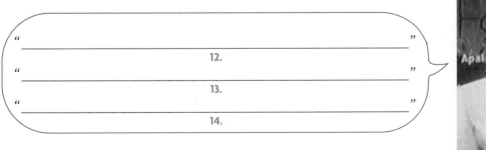

" _____ "
12.
" _____ "
13.
" _____ "
14.

COMMUNICATION PRACTICE

5 LISTENING

Work in groups of four. Listen to the weather advisory. Listen again and check the correct information. It's all right to leave something blank. You're not expected to answer every question. After you listen, you will pool your information.

Schools

1. Today, schools   ☑ closed at 10:00.   ☐ will close at 1:00.

2. Students and teachers   ☐ should stay at school.   ☐ should go home immediately.

3. Tomorrow, schools   ☐ will open.   ☐ may stay closed.

Roads

4. Road conditions   ☐ are safe.   ☐ are dangerous.

5. Drivers must   ☐ drive slowly.   ☐ pick up passengers on the road.

6. Everyone should   ☐ avoid driving.   ☐ continue driving.

Public Offices

7. Libraries   ☐ will stay open.   ☐ will close at 1:00.

8. Post offices   ☐ will stay open until 5:00.   ☐ will close early.

9. Government offices   ☐ will stay closed.   ☐ will remain open tomorrow.

Businesses

10. Banks   ☐ will close at noon.   ☐ will stay open until 3:00.

11. Gas stations   ☐ will close at noon.   ☐ will stay open until evening.

12. Supermarkets   ☐ are open now.   ☐ are closed now.

Now compare your information with what other group members heard. Complete any missing information in your chart. Then listen again and check your work.

EXAMPLE:
A: She said that schools would close at 1:00.
B: That's not right. She said that schools had closed at 10:00.

6 TELEPHONE

Play this game in groups of seven or eight students. One student whispers something in the ear of another student. That student reports (in a whisper) what he or she heard to the next student. Each student must report to the next student in a whisper and may only say the information once. Expect some surprises—people often hear things inaccurately or report them slightly differently from what was actually said. The last student to hear the reported information tells the whole group what he or she heard.

EXAMPLE:
A: There won't be any class tomorrow.
B: He said that there wouldn't be any class tomorrow.
C: She said that there'd be a guest in class tomorrow.

7 INTERVIEW

Use the questions below to interview three people in your class about their experiences. Report your findings to the class.

Have you ever experienced an extreme weather condition or other natural phenomenon such as the following?

a hurricane or typhoon	a flood
very hot weather	a sandstorm
very cold weather	an earthquake
a drought	Other: _____

How did you feel?

What did you do to protect yourself?

What advice would you give to someone in the same situation?

EXAMPLE:
Arielle told me she had experienced a very hot summer when temperatures were over 40°C. She told me that she had felt sick a lot of the time. She said she had stayed indoors until evening every day. Arielle told me that everyone should move slowly and drink a lot of liquids in hot weather.

8 WRITING

Write a paragraph reporting someone else's experience in an extreme weather condition or natural phenomenon. You can use information from your interview in Exercise 7 or you can interview another person.

27 INDIRECT INSTRUCTIONS, COMMANDS, REQUESTS, AND INVITATIONS

GRAMMAR **IN CONTEXT**

BEFORE YOU READ Look at the pictures. Where is the man? What is happening?

Read this transcript of a radio interview with the director of a sleep clinic.

HERE'S TO YOUR HEALTH	TAPE: 56, P. 1

The Snooze News

CONNIE: Good morning! This is Connie Sung, bringing you "Here's to Your Health!," a program about modern health issues. Today we've invited Dr. Ray Thorpe **to talk to us about insomnia**. Dr. Thorpe is the director of the Sleep Disorders Clinic. Welcome to the show!

DR. THORPE: Thanks, Connie. It's great to be here.

CONNIE: Your book *Night Shift* will be coming out soon. In it, you tell people **to pay more attention to sleep disorders**. What's the big deal about losing a little sleep?

DR. THORPE: I always tell people **to think of the biggest industrial disaster that they've ever heard about**. Usually it was caused at least in part by sleep deprivation. Then I ask them **to think about what can happen if they drive when they're tired**. Every year, up to 200,000 automobile accidents are caused by drowsy drivers.

CONNIE: Wow! That *is* a big problem.

DR. THORPE: And a costly one. We figure that fatigue costs businesses about $70 million a year.

CONNIE: That's astounding! But getting back to the personal level, if I come to your clinic, what would you advise me **to do**?

(continued on next page)

DR. THORPE: First, I would find out about some of your habits. If you smoked or drank, I would tell you **to stop**.

CONNIE: Really? A lot of people have a drink to relax.

DR. THORPE: Bad idea. Both habits are not only bad for your general health, but they interfere with sleep.

CONNIE: What about the old-fashioned remedies like warm milk?

DR. THORPE: Actually, a lot of home remedies do make sense. We tell patients **to have a high-carbohydrate snack like a banana before they go to bed**. Warm milk helps, too. But I'd advise you **not to eat a heavy meal before bed**.

CONNIE: My doctor told me **to get more exercise**, but when I run at night, I can't get to sleep.

DR. THORPE: It's true that if you exercise regularly, you'll sleep better. But we always tell patients **not to exercise within three hours of bedtime**.

CONNIE: My mother always said **to get up and scrub the floor when I couldn't sleep**.

DR. THORPE: That works. I advised one patient **to balance his checkbook**. He went right to sleep, just to escape from the task.

CONNIE: Suppose I try these remedies, and they don't help?

DR. THORPE: We often ask patients **to spend a night at our sleep clinic**. We have electronic equipment that permits us to monitor the patient through the night. In fact, if you're interested, we can invite you **to come to the clinic for a night**.

CONNIE: Maybe I should do that.

GRAMMAR **PRESENTATION**
INDIRECT INSTRUCTIONS, COMMANDS, REQUESTS, AND INVITATIONS

	DIRECT SPEECH						INDIRECT SPEECH		
SUBJECT	REPORTING VERB	DIRECT SPEECH			SUBJECT	REPORTING VERB	NOUN / PRONOUN	INDIRECT SPEECH	
He	said,	"**Drink** warm milk."			He	told	Connie	**to drink** warm milk.	
		"**Don't drink** alcohol before bed."				advised		**not to drink** alcohol before bed.	
						asked	her		
		"Can you please **turn out** the light?"				said		**to turn out** the light.	
		"Why don't you **visit** the sleep clinic?"				invited	her	**to visit** the sleep clinic.	

NOTES

1. In indirect speech, use the **infinitive** (*to* + base form of the verb) to report:

  a. instructions

  b. commands

  c. requests

  d. invitations

  (*See Appendix 13 on page A-5 for a list of reporting verbs.*)

EXAMPLES

DIRECT SPEECH | INDIRECT SPEECH
"Come early," said the doctor. | The doctor told her *to come* early.

"Lie down." | The doctor told her *to lie down*.

"Could you please arrive by 8:00?" | He asked her *to arrive* by 8:00.

"Could you join us for dinner?" | They invited us *to join* them for dinner.

2. Use a **negative infinitive** (*not* + infinitive) to report:

  a. negative instructions

  b. negative commands

  c. negative requests

DIRECT SPEECH | INDIRECT SPEECH
"Don't eat after 9:00 P.M." | He told me *not to eat* after 9:00 P.M.

"Don't wake Cindy!" | Michael told me *not to wake* Cindy.

"Please don't set the alarm." | She asked me *not to set* the alarm.

FOCUSED PRACTICE

1 DISCOVER THE GRAMMAR

Connie Sung decided to write an article about her visit to Dr. Thorpe's clinic. Read her notes for the article. Circle the reporting verbs and underline the indirect instructions, commands, requests, and invitations.

2/18	11:00 A.M. The clinic calls and (asks) me to arrive at 8:30 tonight. They tell me to bring my nightshirt and toothbrush. They tell me people also like to bring their own pillow, but I decide to travel light.
	8:30 P.M. I arrive on schedule. My room is small but cozy. Only the video camera and cable tell me I'm in a sleep clinic. Juan Estrada, the technician on duty, tells me to relax and watch TV for an hour.
	9:30 P.M. Juan comes back and gets me ready to sleep. He pastes twelve small metal disks to my face, legs, and stomach. I ask him to explain, and he tells me that the disks, called electrodes, will be connected to a machine that records electrical activity in my brain. I feel like a Martian in a science fiction movie.
	11:30 P.M. Juan comes back and asks me to get into bed. After he hooks me up to the machine, he instructs me not to leave the bed any more that night. I fall asleep easily.
2/19	7:00 A.M. Juan comes to awaken me and to disconnect the wires. He invites me to join him in the next room, where he had spent the night monitoring the equipment. I look at the pages of graphs and wonder aloud whether Juan and Dr. Thorpe will be able to read my weird dream of the night before. Juan laughs and tells me not to worry. "These are just electrical impulses," he assures me.
	8:00 A.M. Dr. Thorpe reviews my data with me. He tells me I have healthy sleep patterns, except for some leg movements during the night. He tells me to get more exercise, and I promise I will.

2 DEAR HELEN

Read the questions to Helen, a newspaper columnist specializing in health matters, and report her instructions. Use the reporting verbs in parentheses.

Q: I have trouble getting to sleep every night.—MIKE LANDERS, DETROIT

A: Don't drink anything with caffeine after 2:00 P.M. Try exercising regularly, early in the day. Read Dr. Thorpe's new book, *Night Shift,* for more tips.

1. (tell) _She told him not to drink anything with caffeine after 2:00 P.M._

2. (say) _She said to try exercising regularly._

3. (tell) _____

Q: Is there anything I can do to soothe a sore throat? I don't like over-the-counter medicines.—ANNE BOYLE, MIAMI

A: Sip some hot herbal tea with honey. But don't drink black tea. Regular black tea contains a chemical that will dry out your throat.

4. (say) _____

5. (tell) _____

Q: I have cramps in my legs every night. They wake me up, and I have trouble getting back to sleep.—LOUISE RICH, DALLAS

A: The next time you feel a cramp, do this: Pinch the place between your upper lip and your nose. The cramp should stop right away.

6. (say) _____

Q: Do you know of an inexpensive way to remove stains on teeth?—PETE LEE, BROOKLYN

A: Make a toothpaste of one tablespoon of baking soda and a little water.

7. (tell) _____

Q: What can I do to ease an itchy poison ivy rash?—MARVIN SMITH, HARTFORD

A: Spread cool, cooked oatmeal over the rash. Also, try soaking the rash in a cool bath with one-fourth cup baking soda. Don't scratch the rash. That will make it worse.

8. (tell) _____

9. (say) _____

10. (tell) _____

Q: Bugs seems to love me. Mosquitoes and gnats bite me much more than other people.—ED SMALL, WASHINGTON, D.C.

A: There are a couple of things you can do to keep the pests away. Eat onions or garlic every day. Your skin will have a slight odor that bugs hate. Or ask your doctor about a vitamin B supplement.

11. (say) _____

12. (tell) _____

Q: What makes a sunburn feel better?—PAM LUKAS, LOS ANGELES

A: Dissolve one-fourth cup of cornstarch in a lukewarm bath. Don't rub your skin with the towel when drying off. Don't use anything containing alcohol on your skin. Alcohol dries skin and makes a sunburn feel worse.

13. (tell) _____

> **IMPORTANT:** CALL YOUR DOCTOR ABOUT ANY CONDITION THAT DOESN'T IMPROVE OR GETS WORSE.

3 EDITING

Read this entry in Zahra's journal. Find and correct eleven mistakes in the use of indirect instructions, commands, requests, and invitations. The first mistake is already corrected. Remember to look at punctuation!

In writing class today, Juan read one of his stories. It was wonderful. After class, the teacher invited me *to* read a story in class next week. However, I asked her no to call on me next week because I'm having trouble getting ideas. She told me that not to worry, and she said to wait for two weeks. Then I talked to Juan, and I asked him tell me the source for his ideas. He said that they came from his dreams, and he said me to keep a dream journal for ideas. He invited me "to read some of his journal." It was very interesting, so I asked him to give me some tips on remembering dreams. He said getting a good night's sleep because the longer dreams come after a long period of sleep. He also tell me to keep my journal by the bed and to write as soon as I wake up. He said to no move from the sleeping position. He also didn't tell me to think about the day at first. (If you think about your day, you might forget your dreams.) Most important—every night he tells himself that to remember his dreams.

4 CONNIE'S DREAM

Connie had a dream at the sleep clinic. She wrote about it in her journal. Read her account of the dream and underline the indirect commands, instructions, requests, and invitations. Then complete the cartoon by writing what each character said.

I dreamed that a Martian came into my room. He told me <u>to get up</u>. Then he said to follow him. There was a spaceship outside the clinic. I asked the Martian to show me the ship, so he invited me to come aboard. Juan, the lab technician, was on the ship. Suddenly, Juan told me to pilot the ship. He ordered me not to leave the controls. Then he went to sleep. Next, Dr. Thorpe was at my side, giving me instructions. He told me to slow down. Then he said to point the ship towards the earth. There was a loud knocking noise as we hit the ground, and I told everyone not to panic. Then I heard Juan tell me to wake up. I opened my eyes and saw him walking into my room at the sleep clinic.

COMMUNICATION PRACTICE

5 LISTENING

Juan went to a headache clinic. Listen to the conversation to find out what he learned there. Then listen again and check the appropriate column to show what they told him to do, what they told him not to do, and what they didn't mention.

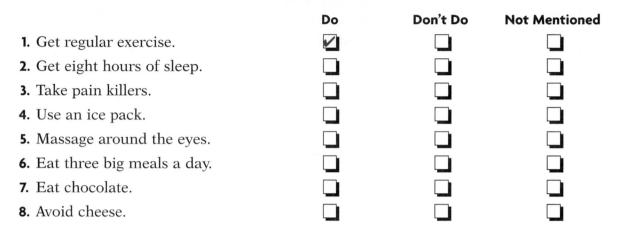

	Do	Don't Do	Not Mentioned
1. Get regular exercise.	☑	☐	☐
2. Get eight hours of sleep.	☐	☐	☐
3. Take pain killers.	☐	☐	☐
4. Use an ice pack.	☐	☐	☐
5. Massage around the eyes.	☐	☐	☐
6. Eat three big meals a day.	☐	☐	☐
7. Eat chocolate.	☐	☐	☐
8. Avoid cheese.	☐	☐	☐

6 SIMPLE REMEDIES

What advice have you heard for the following ailments? Work with a partner and tell what to do and what not to do about these problems. Then report to the class.

minor kitchen burns

insomnia

insect bites

headaches

snoring

hiccups

a cold

blisters

poison ivy

a sore throat

Other: _____

EXAMPLE:

A: My mother always told me to hold a burn under cold water.

B: They say not to put butter on a burn.

7 HOME ALONE

Jeff's parents went out for the evening and left a list of instructions for him. Work with a partner. Read the list and look at the picture. Talk about which instructions Jeff followed and which ones he didn't follow. Use indirect instructions.

Dear Jeff,

We'll be home late. Please follow these instructions:

Don't stay up after 10:00.

Take the garbage out.

Wash the dishes.

Do your homework.

Let the cat in.

Don't watch any horror movies.(They give you nightmares—remember?)

Please don't invite your friends in tonight.

Love,
Mom and Dad

EXAMPLE:

His parents told him not to stay up after 10:00, but it's 11:30 and he's still awake.

8 WRITING

Use the paragraph from Connie's journal in Exercise 4 as a model and write an account of a dream. It can be a dream you had, or one that someone has told you about. You can even invent a dream. Use indirect instructions, commands, requests, and invitations in your writing.

Exchange your paragraph with a partner. Make a sketch of your partner's dream and write the direct speech in speech bubbles. Discuss your drawing with your partner to make sure you understood the story and the indirect speech in your partner's dream.

INDIRECT QUESTIONS

GRAMMAR IN CONTEXT

BEFORE YOU READ Look at the picture. What do you think a stress interview is?

Read this excerpt from an article about job interviews.

The Stress Interview

BY MIGUEL VEGA

A few weeks ago, Melissa Morrow had an unusual job interview. First, the interviewer asked **why she couldn't work under pressure**. Before she could answer, he asked **if she had cleaned out her car recently**. Then he wanted to know **who had written her application letter for her**. Melissa was shocked, but she handled herself well. She asked the interviewer **whether he was going to ask her serious questions**. Then she politely ended the interview.

Melissa had had a stress interview, a type of job interview that features tough, tricky questions, long silences, and negative evaluations of the candidate. To the candidate, this strategy may seem like unnecessary nastiness on the part of the interviewer. However, some positions require an ability to handle just this kind of pressure. If there is an accident in a nuclear power plant, for example, the plant's public relations officer must remain poised when unfriendly reporters ask **how the accident could have occurred**.

(continued on next page)

The Stress Interview (continued)

The hostile atmosphere of a stress interview gives the employer a chance to watch a candidate react to pressure. In one case, the interviewer ended each interview by telling the candidate, "We're really not sure that you're the right person for this job." One very promising candidate asked the interviewer angrily **if he was sure he knew how to conduct an interview**. She clearly could not handle the pressure she would encounter as a television news anchor—the job she was interviewing for.

Stress questioning is not appropriate for all jobs. It may make sense while interviewing a news anchor, but it is unnecessary for less pressured jobs such as accountants, administrative assistants, and computer programmers. Even when it is appropriate, the stress interview can work against a company because some good candidates will refuse the job after a hostile interview. Melissa Morrow handled her interview beautifully, but later asked herself **if she really wanted to work for that company**. Her answer was no.

A word of warning to job candidates: Not all tough questioning constitutes a legitimate stress interview. In some countries like the United States, some questions are illegal unless the answers are directly related to the job. If your interviewer asks **how old you are**, **whether you are married**, or **how much money you owe**, you can refuse to answer. If you think a question is improper, you should ask the interviewer **how the answer specifically relates to that job**. If you don't get a satisfactory explanation, you don't have to answer the question.

When an interviewer introduces pressure to create a reaction, it's easy to lose your cool. Remember that all interviews create stress. If you expect it and learn to control your responses, you can stay poised even in a stress interview.

DID YOU KNOW . . .

In some countries, employers must hire only on the basis of skills and experience. In the United States, for example, an interviewer cannot ask an applicant certain questions unless the information is related to the job. The following are some of the questions an interviewer may not ask:

- How old are you?
- What is your religion?
- Are you married?
- What does your husband (or wife) do?
- Have you ever been arrested?
- How many children do you have?
- How tall are you?
- What country were you born in?

GRAMMAR **PRESENTATION**
INDIRECT QUESTIONS

DIRECT SPEECH: *YES / NO* QUESTIONS		
SUBJECT	REPORTING VERB	DIRECT QUESTION
He	asked,	**"Do you have** any experience**?"** **"Can you use** a computer**?"** **"Will you stay** for a year**?"**

INDIRECT SPEECH: *YES / NO* QUESTIONS				
SUBJECT	REPORTING VERB	(NOUN / PRONOUN)		INDIRECT QUESTION
He	asked	(Melissa) (her)	**if** **whether**	**she had** any experience. **she could use** a computer. **she would stay** for a year.

DIRECT SPEECH: *WH-* QUESTIONS ABOUT THE SUBJECT		
SUBJECT	REPORTING VERB	DIRECT QUESTION
He	asked,	**"Who told you** about the job**?"** **"What happened** on **your** last job**?"** **"How many applied** for the job**?"**

INDIRECT SPEECH: *WH-* QUESTIONS ABOUT THE SUBJECT				
SUBJECT	REPORTING VERB	(NOUN / PRONOUN)		INDIRECT QUESTION
He	asked	(Bob) (him)	**who**	**had told him** about the job.
			what	**had happened** on **his** last job.
			how many	**had applied** for the job.

(continued on next page)

DIRECT SPEECH: *WH-* QUESTIONS ABOUT THE PREDICATE

SUBJECT	REPORTING VERB	DIRECT QUESTION
He	asked,	"Who(m) **did you work** for?" "What **did you do** there?" "When **did you leave?**" "Where **do you work** now?" "How **are you going to get** to work?" "Why **have you decided to change** jobs?" "How much **are you making?**"

INDIRECT SPEECH: *WH-* QUESTIONS ABOUT THE PREDICATE

SUBJECT	REPORTING VERB	(NOUN / PRONOUN)	INDIRECT QUESTION	
He	asked	(Melissa) (her)	who(m)	she had worked for.
			what	she had done there.
			when	she had left.
			where	she worked now.
			how	she was going to get to work.
			why	she had decided to change jobs.
			how much	she was making.

NOTES

1. Use *if* or *whether* in <u>indirect *yes/no* questions</u>.

People often use *whether or not* to report *yes/no* questions.

USAGE NOTE: *Whether* is considered more formal than *if*.

EXAMPLES

DIRECT SPEECH
"Can you type?" she asked.

INDIRECT SPEECH
She asked me *if* **I could type**.

"Do you know how to use a fax machine?" he asked.

He wanted to know *whether* **I knew how to use a fax machine**.

• He wanted to know *whether or not* **I knew how to use a fax machine**.

2. Use **question words** in <u>indirect *wh-* questions</u>.

DIRECT SPEECH	INDIRECT SPEECH
"Where is your office?" I asked.	I asked *where* **his office was**.
I asked, "How much is the salary?"	I asked *how much* **the salary was**.

3. BE CAREFUL! Use **statement word order**, not question word order, for indirect *yes/no* questions and for indirect *wh-* questions about the predicate.

Notice that indirect questions:

a. do not use the auxiliary *do, does,* or *did.*

b. <u>end with a period</u> (not a question mark).

DIRECT SPEECH	INDIRECT SPEECH
He asked, "Does the company provide good benefits?"	He asked *whether* **the company provided** good benefits. NOT ~~He asked does the company provide good benefits.~~
"Why did you leave your previous job?" she asked.	She asked me *why* **I had left** my previous job. NOT ~~She asked me why did I leave my previous job?~~

4. For indirect *wh-* questions about the subject, keep <u>the same word order as direct questions</u>.

DIRECT SPEECH	INDIRECT SPEECH
"Who got the job?" I asked.	I asked *who* **had gotten the job**.
"What caused the problem?" I asked.	I asked *what* **had caused the problem**.

REFERENCE NOTES
The same verb tense changes and other changes occur in indirect questions as in indirect statements. *(See Units 25 and 26).*
For a list of verbs used to report questions, see Appendix 13 on page A-5.

FOCUSED PRACTICE

1 DISCOVER THE GRAMMAR

Melissa Morrow is telling a friend about her job interview. Underline the indirect questions in the conversation.

DON: So, how did the interview go?

MELISSA: It was very strange.

DON: What happened?

MELISSA: Well, it started off like a normal interview. He asked me <u>how much experience I had had</u>, and I told him I had been a public relations officer for ten years. Let's see. . . . He also asked what I would change about my current job. That was a little tricky.

DON: What did you say?

MELISSA: Well, I didn't want to say anything negative, so I told him that I was ready for more responsibility.

DON: Good. What else did he ask?

MELISSA: Oh, you know, the regular things. He asked when I had been most successful, and how much money I was making.

DON: Sounds like a normal interview to me. What was so strange about it?

MELISSA: Well, at one point, he just stopped talking for a long time. Then he asked me all these bizarre questions that weren't even related to the job.

DON: Like what?

MELISSA: He asked me if I had cleaned out my car recently.

DON: You're kidding.

MELISSA: No, I'm not. Then he asked me why my employer didn't want me to stay.

DON: That's crazy. I hope you told him that you hadn't been fired.

MELISSA: Of course. Oh, and he asked if I was good enough to work for his company.

DON: What did you tell him?

MELISSA: I told him that with my skills and experience I was one of the best in my field.

DON: That was a great answer. It sounds like you handled yourself very well.

MELISSA: Thanks. But now I'm asking myself if I really want this job.

DON: Take your time. Don't make any snap decisions.

Now check the direct questions that Melissa was asked.

☑ **1.** How much experience have you had?

☐ **2.** What would you change about your current job?

☐ **3.** Are you ready for more responsibility?

☐ **4.** When were you most successful?

☐ **5.** How much are you making now?

☐ **6.** Was it a normal interview?

☐ **7.** Have you cleaned out your car recently?

☐ **8.** Have you been fired?

☐ **9.** Are you good enough to work for this company?

☐ **10.** Do you ever make any snap decisions?

2 **NOSY NEIGHBOR**   **Grammar Notes 1–4**

Claire has an interview next week. Her neighbor, Jaime, wants to know all about it. Report Jaime's questions, using the words in parentheses.

JAIME: I heard you're going on an interview next week. What kind of job is it?

CLAIRE: It's for a job as an office assistant.

1.   He asked what kind of job it was. _____
                        (kind of job / what / was / it)

JAIME: Oh, really? When is the interview?

CLAIRE: It's on Tuesday at 9:00.

2. _____
                        (the interview / was / when)

JAIME: Where's the company?

CLAIRE: It's downtown on the west side.

3. _____
                        (was / where / the company)

JAIME: Do you need directions?

CLAIRE: No, I know the way.

4. _____
                        (needed / if / she / directions)

JAIME: How long does it take to get there?

CLAIRE: About half an hour.

5. _____
                        (to get there / it / takes / how long)

JAIME: Are you going to drive?

CLAIRE: I think so. It's probably the fastest way.

6. _____
                        (was going / if / she / to drive)

(continued on next page)

JAIME: Who's going to interview you?

CLAIRE: Uhmm. I'm not sure. Probably the manager of the department.

7. _____

(was going / her / who / to interview)

JAIME: Well, good luck. When will they let you know?

CLAIRE: It will take a while. They have a lot of candidates.

8. _____

(her / they / would / when / let / know)

3 WHO'S ASKING? Grammar Notes 1–5

*Read the following questions, which were asked during Claire Yang's interview.
Some were asked by Claire, and some were asked by the manager, Pete Stollins.
Decide who asked each question. Then rewrite each question as indirect speech.*

1. "What type of training is available for the job?"

   Claire asked what type of training was available for the job.

2. "What kind of experience do you have?"

   Pete asked what kind of experience she had.

3. "Is there opportunity for promotion?"

   _____

4. "Are you interviewing with other companies?"

   _____

5. "What will my responsibilities be?"

   _____

6. "How is job performance rewarded?"

   _____

7. "What was your starting salary at your last job?"

   _____

8. "Did you get along well with your last employer?"

   _____

9. "Do you hire many women?"

   _____

10. "Were you fired from your last job?"

   _____

11. "Why did you apply for this position?"

_____

12. "Have you had any major layoffs in the past few years?"

_____

4 EDITING

Read part of a memo an interviewer wrote after an interview. Find and correct seven mistakes in the use of indirect questions. The first mistake is already corrected. Remember to look at punctuation!

May 15, 2000

To: Francesca Giuffrida

From: Bob Marley

Subject: Interview with Carl Treng

This morning I interviewed Carl Treng for the administrative assistant position. Since this job requires a lot of contact with the public, I did some stress questioning. I asked Mr. Treng why ~~couldn't he~~ *he couldn't* work under pressure. I also asked him why his supervisor disliked him. Finally, I inquired when he would quit the job with our company?

Mr. Treng kept his poise throughout the interview. He answered all my questions calmly, and he had some excellent questions of his own. He asked "if we expected changes in the job." He also wanted to know how often do we evaluate employees. I was quite impressed when he asked why did I decide to join this company.

Mr. Treng is an excellent candidate for the job, and I believe he will handle the responsibilities well. At the end of the interview, Mr. Treng inquired when we could let him know our decision? I asked him if whether he was considering another job, and he said he was. I think we should act quickly to hire Mr. Treng.

COMMUNICATION PRACTICE

5 LISTENING

You are going to hear a job interview that takes place in the United States. Before you listen, read the chart. Then listen to the interview and check the topics the interviewer asks about.

SOME TOPICS YOU MIGHT BE ASKED ABOUT DURING A JOB INTERVIEW

OK to Ask

- ☐ Name
- ☐ Address
- ☐ Work experience
- ☐ Reason for leaving job
- ☑ Reason for seeking position that is open
- ☐ Salary
- ☐ Education
- ☐ Professional organizations
- ☐ Convictions for crimes
- ☐ Skills
- ☐ Job performance
- ☐ Permission to work in the United States

Not OK to Ask
(illegal if not related to the job)

- ☑ Age
- ☐ Race
- ☐ Sex
- ☐ Religion
- ☐ National origin
- ☐ Height or weight
- ☐ Marital status
- ☐ Information about spouse
- ☐ Arrest record
- ☐ Physical disabilities
- ☐ Children
- ☐ Citizenship
- ☐ English language skill
- ☐ Financial situation

Listen again and note the illegal questions the interviewer asks.

1. How old are you?
2. _____
3. _____
4. _____
5. _____
6. _____
7. _____

Report the illegal questions to your classmates.

EXAMPLE:
He asked her how old she was.

6 ROLE PLAY

Work in groups. Using the ad and the résumé, develop questions for a job interview. Half of the group should write questions for the interviewer, and the other half should write questions for the candidate. Then select two people in your group to act out the interview for the whole class.

Pat Rogers
215 West Hill Drive
Baltimore, MD 21233
Telephone: (410) 555-7777

MEDICAL RECEPTIONIST for busy doctor's office. Mature individual needed to answer phones, greet patients, make appointments, some filing and billing. Similar experience preferred. Computer skills a plus.

EDUCATION	**Taylor Community College** Associate's Degree (Business) 1996 **Middlesex High School** High school diploma, 1993
EXPERIENCE 1996–2000 **Patients Plus** **Baltimore, MD**	**Medical receptionist** Responsibilities: Greeted patients, made appointments, answered telephones, typed medical records using computer.
1993–1996 **Union Hospital** **Baltimore, MD**	**Admitting clerk, hospital admissions office** Responsibilities: Interviewed patients for admission, entered information in computer, answered telephones.

After each role play, discuss the interview as a class. Use the following questions to guide your discussion. Support your ideas by reporting questions that were asked in the interview.

1. Was it a stress interview? Why or why not?

2. Did the interviewer ask any illegal questions? Which ones were illegal?

3. Which of the candidate's questions were the most useful in evaluating the job? Explain your choices.

4. Which of the interviewer's questions gave the clearest picture of the candidate? Explain your choices.

5. If you were the interviewer, would you hire this candidate? Why or why not?

6. If you were the candidate, would you want to work for this company? Why or why not?

EXAMPLE:
I think it was a stress interview because the interviewer asked him why he couldn't find a job.

The interviewer asked two illegal questions. She asked when the candidate was born. She also asked where the candidate was from.

7 CURIOUS QUESTIONS

Work with a partner. What would you like to know about him or her? Make a list of questions. Ask and answer each other's questions. Then get together with another pair and report your conversations.

EXAMPLE:

She asked me what I was going to do next semester. I told her I was going to take the advanced-level ESL class.

8 IN YOUR EXPERIENCE

In small groups, discuss a personal experience with a school or job interview. It could be your own experience, or the experience of someone you know. Talk about these questions:

What did the interviewer want to find out?

What was the most difficult question to answer? Why?

Were there any questions that you didn't want to answer? What did you say?

What did you ask the interviewer?

9 WRITING

Before you look for work, it's a good idea to talk to people who are already working in jobs you might want to do. In these "informational interviews" you can ask what the tasks in that job are, why people like or dislike the work, or how much you can expect to be paid.

Write a list of questions to ask in an informational interview about a job. Then interview someone and write a report about the interview. Use indirect questions.

EXAMPLE:

I interviewed Pete Ortiz, who is an assistant in the computer lab. I wanted to talk to him because I'm interested in applying for a job in the lab. I asked Pete if he liked working there, and he told me he liked it most of the time. . . .

EMBEDDED QUESTIONS

GRAMMAR **IN CONTEXT**

BEFORE YOU READ   Look at the picture. What is the couple worried about?

 *Read an interview about tipping.*

he Tip

In China it used to be illegal, in New Zealand it's uncommon, and in Germany it's included in the bill. In the United States and Canada it's common but illogical: You tip the person who delivers flowers, but not the person who delivers a package. So what's a person to do?

Our correspondent, Marjorie S. Fuchs, interviewed Irene Frankel, author of *Tips on Tipping,* to help us through the tipping maze.

The service was terrible! I wonder if we should leave a tip.

I am not sure whether service is included or not.

I wonder what kind of tip these guys are going to leave.

MSF: Tell me **why you decided to write a book about tipping.**

IF: I began writing it for people from cultures where tipping wasn't a custom. But when I started researching, I found that Americans had a lot of questions also, so *Tips* became a book for anybody living in the United States.

MSF: Does your book explain **who to tip?**

IF: Oh, absolutely. It tells you **who to tip, how much to tip, and when to tip.** Equally important, it tells you **when not to tip.**

MSF: That *is* important. Suppose I don't know **whether to tip someone,** and I left your book at home. Is it OK to ask?

IF: Sure. If you don't know **whether to leave a tip,** the best thing to do is ask. People usually won't tell you **what to do,** but they *will* tell you **what most customers do.**

MSF: I always wonder **what to do when I get bad service.** Should I still tip?

IF: Don't tip the ordinary amount, but tip *something* so that the service person doesn't think that you just forgot to leave a tip.

(continued on next page)

The Tip (continued)

MSF: Is there any reason **why we tip a restaurant server but not a flight attendant?**

IF: Not that I know. The rules for tipping in the United States are very illogical, and there are often contradictions in who we tip. That's why I wrote this book.

MSF: Another thing—I've never understood **why a restaurant tip depends on the amount of the bill rather than on the amount of work involved in serving the meal.** After all, bringing out a $20 dish of food involves the same amount of work as carrying out a $5 plate.

IF: You're right. It makes no sense. That's just the way it is.

MSF: One last question. Suppose I'm planning a trip to Egypt. Tell me **how I can learn about tipping customs in that country.**

IF: Usually travel agents know **what the rules are for tipping in each country.** Call the consulate if you can't find out from a travel agent or a book.

MSF: Well, thanks for all the good tips. I know our readers will find them very helpful. *I certainly did.*

IF: Thank *you.*

TIPPING AT A SALON

GRAMMAR **PRESENTATION**
EMBEDDED QUESTIONS

MAIN CLAUSE	EMBEDDED QUESTION
I'm not sure He wondered	**if I left the right tip.** **whether five dollars was enough.**
Can you remember	**how much our bill was?**

	WH- WORD + INFINITIVE
I don't know	**how much to tip.**
Do you know	**where to leave the tip?**

NOTES

EXAMPLES

1. In Unit 28, you learned to use **indirect questions** to <u>report another person's words</u>.

Indirect questions are a kind of **embedded question**. An embedded question is one that is <u>included within another sentence</u>. This unit discusses embedded questions that <u>do not report another person's words</u>.

DIRECT QUESTION
Did you leave a tip?

INDIRECT QUESTION
Michael asked **if I had left a tip.**

EMBEDDED QUESTION
Do you remember **if I left a tip?**

2. Embedded questions can be <u>inside a statement or inside another question</u>.

- I don't know **who our server is.**
  (The main sentence is the statement I don't know . . .)
- Do you remember **who our server is?**
  (The main sentence is the question Do you remember . . . ?)

▶ **BE CAREFUL!** If the embedded question is <u>in a statement</u>, use a <u>period</u> at the end of the sentence.

If the embedded question is <u>in a question</u>, use a <u>question mark</u> at the end of the sentence.

- I wonder **if that's our server.**
  NOT ~~I wonder if that's our server?~~
- Do you know **if that's our server?**

(continued on next page)

3. We often **use embedded questions** to
a. express something we do not know.

DIRECT QUESTION	EMBEDDED QUESTION
Why didn't he tip the mechanic?	I don't know **why he didn't tip the mechanic.**

b. ask politely for information.

Is the tip included?	Can you tell me **if the tip is included?**

USAGE NOTE: When we approach people we don't know, or in formal situations, it is considered more polite to use an embedded question than a direct question.

Less formal:	*More polite:*
Does our bill include a service charge?	Can you tell me **if our bill includes a service charge?**

4. Introduce **embedded *yes/no* questions** with *if, whether,* or *whether or not*.

- Do you know *if* **they delivered the pizza?**

  OR

- Do you know *whether* **they delivered the pizza?**

  OR

- Do you know *whether or not* **they delivered the pizza?**

USAGE NOTE: ***Whether*** is considered more formal than *if*.

Introduce **embedded *wh-* questions** with a question word.

- Many tourists wonder *how much* **they should tip their restaurant server.**

5. BE CAREFUL!

a. Use **statement word order**, not question word order, in embedded *wh-* questions about the predicate and in embedded *yes/no* questions.

Do not leave out *if* or *whether* in embedded *yes/no* questions.

DIRECT QUESTION	EMBEDDED QUESTION
What time is it?	Could you tell me *what time* **it is?** NOT ~~Could you tell me what time is it?~~
Is it 6:00 yet?	Could you tell me *if* **it is** 6:00 yet? NOT ~~Could you tell me is it 6:00 yet?~~

b. Do not use the auxiliary verbs *do, does,* or *did* in embedded questions.

- I don't know **when the pizza came**. NOT I don't know ~~when did the pizza come~~.

6. In embedded questions, you can also use the **infinitive** <u>after a question word or whether</u>.

- Could you explain how I should figure out the tip?

  OR

- Could you explain *how* **to figure out** the tip?

- I don't know whether I should leave a tip.

  OR

- I don't know *whether* **to leave a tip**.

▶ **BE CAREFUL!** Do not use the infinitive after *if* or *why*.

- I don't understand *why* **I should tip**. NOT ~~I don't understand why to tip.~~

7. Embedded questions often **follow certain phrases**:

I don't know . . . .
I'd like to know . . . .
Do you know . . . ?
Can you tell me . . . ?
I can't remember . . . .
Can you remember . . . ?
Let's ask . . . .
We need to find out . . . .
I'd like to find out . . . .
I wonder . . . .
I'm not sure . . . .
It doesn't say . . . .
Could you explain . . . ?
I can't imagine . . . .

- *I don't know* what the name of the restaurant is.

- *Can you remember* how much the shrimp costs?

- *Let's ask* what today's specials are.

- *I wonder* what time the restaurant closes.

- *Could you explain* what that sign means?

- *I can't imagine* why this restaurant isn't more popular.

FOCUSED PRACTICE

1 DISCOVER THE GRAMMAR

Read the ad for Tips on Tipping. *Underline the embedded questions.*

Tips on Tipping

This book is for you if . . .

you've ever avoided a situation just because you didn't know <u>how much to tip.</u>

you've ever realized (too late) that you were supposed to offer a tip.

you've ever given a huge tip and then wondered if a tip was necessary at all.

you've ever needed to know how to calculate the right tip instantly.

you're new to the United States and you're not sure who you should tip here.

you'd like to learn how tipping properly can get you the best service for your money.

What readers are saying . . .

"I can't imagine how I got along without it."
　—*Chris Sarton, Minneapolis*

"Take *Tips* along if you want a stress-free vacation."
　—*Midori Otaka, Osaka, Japan*

"I took my fiancée to dinner at Deux Saisons and knew exactly how to tip everyone!"
　—*S. Prasad, San Francisco*

"You need this book—whether you stay in hostels or five-star hotels."
　—*Cuno Pumpin, Bern, Switzerland*

Send for the ultimate guide to tipping and have all these questions answered.

- ✂ - - - - - - - - -

Yes! I want to learn who to tip, when to tip, and how much to tip. Please send me _____ copies of *Tips on Tipping*. I'm enclosing $4.95 plus $2.00 postage and handling for each book. (New Jersey residents: Add sales tax.) Don't forget to include your address and ZIP code.

I've enclosed my check or money order for $_____ made payable to

Martin Unlimited, Inc.
P.O. Box 2075
Hoboken, New Jersey 07030

2 SERVICE CHARGES **Grammar Notes 1–5 and 7**

Complete the travel column about international tipping customs. Change the direct questions in parentheses to embedded questions. Use correct punctuation.

Tipping customs vary, so travelers should find out who, where, and how much to tip. Here are some frequently asked questions.

Q: Can you tell me whether ___I should tip in Canada?___
1. (Should I tip in Canada?)

A: Yes. Tipping practices in Canada are similar to those in the United States.

Q: I know that some places in France include a service charge. Could you explain

_____
2. (How can I tell if the tip is included in the bill?)

A: Look for the phrase *service compris* (service included) on the bill.

Q: I'm going to China next month. I understand that tipping used to be illegal. Please

suggest _____
3. (What can I do instead?)

A: You can give a small gift or you could leave a tip.

Q: On a recent trip to Iceland I found that service people refused tips. Could you explain

_____
4. (Why did this happen?)

A: In Iceland people often feel insulted by tips. Just say thank you—that's enough.

Q: Our family is planning a trip to Norway to visit my in-laws. My daughter wants to take

some skiing lessons while we're there. I'd like to know _____
5. (Should I tip her instructor?)

A: Tipping is rare all over Scandinavia. Take the instructor to lunch instead.

Q: I'm going to work in Japan for a year. I'm bringing a lot of luggage. Could you tell me

_____
6. (How much should I tip the airport and train porters?)

A: There's a fixed fee per bag for airport porters. No tipping is expected on trains.

Q: My husband and I are planning a trip to Australia. Please tell us

_____
7. (Who expects a tip and who doesn't?)

A: Restaurant servers expect a tip of ten percent, but you don't need to tip taxi drivers.

3 **TOURISTS**

Two foreign exchange students are visiting Washington, D.C. Complete their conversations. Choose the appropriate questions from the box and change them to embedded questions. Remember to correctly punctuate the sentences.

How much are we supposed to tip the taxi driver?

Could we rent a car and drive there?

Do they have tour buses that go there?

How much does the metro cost?

How far are you going?

How are we going to choose?

How much does a bus tour cost?

What did they put in the sauce?

Where is the Smithsonian Museum?

~~Where is it?~~

Where do they sell them?

1. **DRIVER:** Where do you want to go? Airport?

   MARTINA: The Hotel Edison. Do you know ___where it is?___
   a.

   DRIVER: Sure. Get in and I'll take you there.

   MARTINA: *(whispering to Miuki)* Do you know _____
   b.

   MIUKI: According to the book, we're supposed to leave 10–15 percent. I've got it.

2. **MARTINA:** There's so much to see in Washington. I don't know _____
   a.

   MIUKI: We could take a bus tour of the city first, and then decide.

   MARTINA: Does the guidebook say _____
   b.

   MIUKI: Yeah. About $15 per person, plus tips for the guide and the driver.

3. **MARTINA:** That was delicious.

   MIUKI: Let's try to find out _____
   a.

   MARTINA: It tasted like it had garlic and ginger. I'll ask the waiter.

4. **MARTINA:** Excuse me. Can you tell me _____
   a.

   OFFICER: Sure. Just turn right at the corner and go straight.

5. MARTINA: Let's take the metro. Do you know _____
a.

   MARTINA: It's not expensive. I think it depends on _____
b.

   But we have to get tickets, and I'm not sure _____
c.

   MIUKI: Oh. Probably right in the station.

6. MARTINA: I'd like to visit Williamsburg, Virginia, while we're here.

   MIUKI: I wonder _____
a.

   MARTINA: I'm sure they do, but do you think _____
b.

   MIUKI: Let's do that. We can drive back along the shore.

4 ASKING FOR ADVICE   Grammar Note 6

Complete the conversation. Use a question word and the infinitive form of the verbs in the box.

figure out	get	go	invite	leave	~~wear~~

MARTINA: I can't decide _____ what to wear _____ Friday night.
1.

   MIUKI: Your red dress. You always look great in it. By the way, where are you going?

MARTINA: John's Grill with Janek. We're meeting there at 7:00.

   MIUKI: Great! You know _____ there, don't you?
2.

MARTINA: Yes, but I'm not sure _____.
3.

   MIUKI: Leave at 6:00. That'll give you enough time.

MARTINA: I'd like to take Janek someplace for dessert afterward, but I don't know

_____.
4.

   MIUKI: The desserts at John's are supposed to be pretty good.

MARTINA: Oh. By the way, it's Janek's birthday, so I'm paying. But I'm still not quite sure

_____ the tip.
5.

   MIUKI: Just double the tax. That comes to about 15 percent. So, who else is going?

MARTINA: Well, I thought about asking a few people to join us, but I really didn't know

_____
6.

   MIUKI: Don't worry. I'm sure it will be fine with just the two of you.

COMMUNICATION PRACTICE

⑤ LISTENING

A travel agent is being interviewed on a call-in radio show. The topic is tipping. Listen to the callers' questions. Then listen again, and for each question decide on an appropriate response.

1. **ⓐ** Between 15 and 20 percent of the total bill.
   b. The waiter.

2. **a.** About 15 percent of the fare.
   b. Only if you are happy with the ride.

3. **a.** Before you leave.
   b. On the table.

4. **a.** The person who takes you to your seat.
   b. 20 francs.

5. **a.** The manager.
   b. Don't leave a tip.

6. **a.** $1.00.
   b. At the cashier.

7. **a.** Call the consulate.
   b. It's included in the bill.

8. **a.** $1.00.
   b. Give something to the person who delivers your food.

⑥ TIPPING

Work in small groups. Discuss these questions.

1. Do you think tipping is a good system? Why or why not?
2. Were you ever in a situation where you didn't know what to do about a tip?
3. How is tipping different in the United States and other countries you know?

> **EXAMPLE:**
> **A:** I'm not sure whether tipping is good or not. I think people should get paid enough so that they don't have to depend on tips.
> **B:** I wonder if you would still get good service if the tip were included.
> **C:** Sure you would. A service charge is included in a lot of countries, and the service is still good.

7 INFORMATION GAP: EATING OUT

Work in groups of three (A, B, and C). Students A and B are customers in a restaurant. Student C, you are the server. Turn to page 423 and follow the instructions there. Students A and B, look at the menu below.

John's Grill

MAIN DISHES

APPETIZERS

Soup of the day $2.95
Caesar salad $3.25
John's salad $2.95

Fish

Catch of the day *(please ask waiter)* price varies
Filet of sole with sauce Dijon $8.95
Fried shrimp $9.95

Chicken

Chicken à la John $7.95
Half roast chicken $6.95

Beef

Steak frites $8.95
John's hamburger deluxe $5.95

BEVERAGES

Soda $ .95
Coffee or tea $1.15

Pasta

Macaroni and cheese $5.95
Spaghetti à la John $6.95

DESSERTS

Fruit pie *(in season)* $1.95
Fruit pie à la mode $2.25
Chocolate cake $1.95
Fresh fruit salad $2.95
Dessert of the day
(ask your waiter)

Prices include tax.
Service not included.

All main courses (except pasta) come with your choice of baked potato or fries and the vegetable of the day.

Student A, you are allergic to tomatoes and dairy products. Student B, you don't eat meat or chicken. Discuss the menu with your partner. Then ask your server about items on the menu and order a meal. When you get the check, figure out a 15 percent tip.

EXAMPLE:

A: I wonder what the soup of the day is.

B: Me too. Do you know what's in a Caesar salad?

A: Not really. We'll have to ask the server.
Excuse me. Can you tell us what's in the Caesar salad?

C: Sure. It has lettuce, parmesan cheese, and croutons.

A: Croutons? I don't know what they are.

C: They're toasted cubes of bread.

8 THE FIRST TIME IS ALWAYS THE HARDEST

Think about the first time you did something—for example, the first time you

> drove a car
> went on a job interview
> traveled to a foreign country
> became a parent

What problems did you have? Tell a classmate.

EXAMPLE:

I remember the first time I drove a car. I didn't know how to start it. I didn't know which gear to use. I even had to ask how to turn the windshield wipers on. . . .

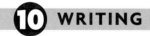

9 ROLE PLAY

Student A, you are a desk clerk at a hotel. Student B, you are a guest at the hotel. Use embedded questions to find out information about the following:

- restaurants
- interesting sights
- transportation
- entertainment
- banks
- shopping
- tipping
- laundry

EXAMPLE:

A: Can I help you?

B: Yes. Could you tell me where to find a good, inexpensive restaurant around here?

A: There are some nice restaurants around the university.

10 WRITING

Think about a time you were traveling. Write about a situation that confused or surprised you. Use embedded questions.

EXAMPLE:

When I was an exchange student in China, my Chinese friends always wanted to know how old I was. I couldn't understand why new friends needed to know my age. I wasn't sure whether to tell the truth, because I was a little younger than everyone else. . . .

INFORMATION GAP FOR STUDENT C

Read these notes about today's menu. Answer your customers' questions. When they are done ordering, look at the menu on page 421 and write a check.

APPETIZERS

Soup of the day

Monday:	*vegetable soup (carrots, peas, string beans in a tomato broth)*
Tuesday:	*tomato soup*
Wednesday:	*pea soup*
Thursday:	*onion soup*
Friday:	*fish soup*
Saturday:	*potato soup*

Caesar salad *(lettuce, parmesan cheese, croutons—toasted bread cubes)*

John's salad *(spinach, mushrooms, tomatoes, onions)*

MAIN DISHES

Catch of the day: *broiled flounder ($6.95)*

Filet of sole with sauce Dijon *(mustard sauce)*

Chicken à la John *(chicken baked in a cream sauce with olives and nuts)*

Steak frites *(steak cooked in pan with butter, served with french fried potatoes)*

John's hamburger deluxe *(hamburger with tomatoes, onions, mushrooms, and cheese)*

Spaghetti à la John *(spaghetti with spinach, fresh tomatoes, and mushrooms in a light cream sauce)*

Vegetable of the day: *broccoli*

DESSERTS

Pies *(cherry, apple, blueberry)*

à la mode *(Ice cream: chocolate, strawberry, vanilla)*

Fruit salad *(apples, bananas, and strawberries)*

Dessert of the day: *strawberry shortcake (yellow cake with fresh strawberries and whipped cream—$2.25)*

EXAMPLE:

A: I wonder what the soup of the day is.

B: Me too. Do you know what's in a Caesar salad?

A: Not really. We'll have to ask the server.
Excuse me. Can you tell us what's in the Caesar salad?

C: Sure. It has lettuce, parmesan cheese, and croutons.

A: Croutons? I don't know what they are.

C: They're toasted cubes of bread.

REVIEW OR SELFTEST

I. *Karen and Jon had a party a week ago. Karen is telling a friend about the conversations she had before the party. Read what people actually said. Then circle the correct words to complete each reported sentence.*

1. "We'd like you and Bill to come to a party at our apartment this Friday."

   I invited Maria and Bill came / (to come) to a party at our apartment
                            a.

   last / this Friday.
     b.

2. "It'll be a housewarming for our new apartment."

   I told them it would be / will be a housewarming for our / their new
                 a.   **b.**

   apartment.

3. "We'll be a little late."

   They said / told me that they / we would be a little late.
        a.   **b.**

4. "What time is your party going to start?"

   Sheila said / asked what time our party is / was going to start.
          a.   **b.**

5. "Should I bring something?"

   She asked if I / she should bring / should have brought something.
            a.   **b.**

6. "Thanks, but that's OK. Don't bring anything."

   I thanked her, but I told / said her not to bring / didn't bring anything.
                a.   **b.**

7. "I've been planning to call you for a long time."

   Tory told me he's been planning / 'd been planning to call us / you for a
                         a.   **b.**

   long time.

8. "I don't know how to get to your place."

   He said he didn't know how / doesn't know how to get to your / our place.
                  a.   **b.**

9. "Is there a bus stop nearby?"

   He said / asked was there / if there was a bus stop nearby.
       a.   **b.**

10. "Don't be afraid of getting lost."

    I told him not to be / be afraid of getting lost.
             a.

11. "Take the Woodmere Avenue bus."

    I <u>invited / told</u> him <u>take / to take</u> the Woodmere Avenue bus.
       a.   b.

12. "I can't come tomorrow night."

    Nita said that she <u>can't / couldn't</u> come <u>the following night / tomorrow night</u>.
                          a.   b.

13. "My cousin from Detroit is arriving today."

    She told me her cousin from Detroit <u>is / was</u> arriving <u>today / that day</u>.
                                            a.   b.

14. "Bring your cousin along."

    I <u>said / told</u> her to bring <u>her / your</u> cousin along.
       a.   b.

15. "The weather bureau has issued a storm warning for tonight."

    Jon told me that the weather bureau <u>has issued / had issued</u> a storm warning for
                                            a.

    <u>tonight / that night</u>.
       b.

16. "Schools will close early today."

    The forecaster said that schools <u>would / will</u> close early <u>today / that day</u>.
                                         a.   b.

17. "Motorists must drive with extreme caution."

    She said that motorists <u>must have driven / had to drive</u> with extreme caution.
                               a.

18. "I love snow."

    Jon always <u>tell / says</u> that he <u>loves / loved</u> snow.
                  a.   b.

19. "Would you please shovel the driveway?"

    The next morning I asked <u>you / him</u> <u>to shovel / if he had shoveled</u> the driveway.
                                a.   b.

20. "Where are my boots?"

    He <u>told / asked</u> me where <u>were his boots / his boots were</u>.
        a.   b.

II. *Each sentence has four underlined words or phrases. The four underlined parts of the sentences are marked A, B, C, or D. Circle the letter of the <u>one</u> underlined word or phrase that is NOT CORRECT.*

1. I <u>wonder</u> <u>how much</u> <u>should I</u> <u>tip</u> the driver for a trip to the airport.   A B Ⓒ D
      A   B   C   D

2. Bob <u>said</u> <u>don't</u> forget <u>to bring</u> my bathing suit <u>because</u> they have a pool.   A B C D
         A   B   C   D

3. The <u>forecaster</u> <u>said,</u> <u>"The</u> weather <u>was going</u> to be great tomorrow."   A B C D
          A   B   C   D

(continued on next page)

4. <u>Cindy asked</u> Paz <u>if there was</u> a telephone in the restaurant or <u>if</u>
    A   B   C

    <u>should she</u> use the car phone.   A B C D
      D

5. She <u>wasn't sure</u> <u>if</u> or not <u>she</u> <u>needed</u> an umbrella.   A B C D
            A   B   C   D

6. The bus driver <u>said</u> me I <u>should</u> <u>get off</u> at Pine Street and <u>walk</u> to Oak. A B C D
              A   B   C   D

7. Juan <u>said</u> that <u>if</u> he <u>had known</u>, he <u>would</u> told me the way.   A B C D
      A   B   C   D

8. <u>When</u> I <u>talked</u> to Pat last month, she <u>told</u> she <u>was leaving</u>.   A B C D
    A   B   C   D

9. It <u>was snowing</u> last night when Vick <u>called</u> me from Florida and <u>told</u> A B C D
      A   B   C

    me he loved the warm weather down <u>here</u>.
                                  D

10. My doctor <u>told me</u> <u>to</u> <u>wearing</u> a hat whenever I <u>go</u> into the sun.   A B C D
            A   B   C   D

III. *Read the direct speech. Circle the letter of the correct word(s) to complete the same speech* ***reported the following day.***

1. "You look beautiful in that dress."   A B C Ⓓ
    She told me _____ beautiful in that dress.
    (A) you look   **(C)** I'll look
    (B) you looked   **(D)** I looked

2. "Have you met Bill and Maria yet?"   A B C D
    Harry asked me _____ Bill and Maria yet.
    (A) if I met   **(C)** did I meet
    (B) have I met   **(D)** if I had met

3. "Is Tory coming tonight?"   A B C D
    I asked Jon _____ Tory was coming that night.
    (A) whether   **(C)** when
    (B) did   **(D)** is

4. "I'm not sure."   A B C D
    He told me _____ sure.
    (A) I wasn't   **(C)** he isn't
    (B) he wasn't   **(D)** I'm not

5. "Why don't you ride home with us?"   A B C D
    Bill invited me _____ home with them.
    (A) why I didn't ride   **(C)** to ride
    (B) not to ride   **(D)** riding

6. "It may snow tonight."   A B C D
    He said it might snow _____.
    (A) tomorrow night   **(C)** at night
    (B) that night   **(D)** tonight

7. "Call me tomorrow."   **A B C D**

Karen said _____ her the next day.

(A) to call   (C) call

(B) me to call   (D) I will call

8. "We ought to get together more often."   **A B C D**

We all said that we _____ together more often.

(A) had better get   (C) ought to get

(B) ought to have gotten   (D) should have gotten

9. "Don't drive fast."   **A B C D**

Jon told Maria _____ fast.

(A) to not drive   (C) they don't drive

(B) don't drive   (D) not to drive

10. "I had a great time."   **A B C D**

Bill told Jon _____ had had a great time.

(A) I   (C) you

(B) he   (D) Jon

IV. *Report the conversation that Nita and Jon had at the party last week.*

1. NITA: How long have you and Karen been living here?

(ask)   Nita asked how long Jon and Karen had been living there.

2. JON: We moved in three weeks ago.

(tell) _____

3. NITA: Do you like this place better than your old apartment?

(ask) _____

4. JON: We like it a lot more.

(say) _____

5. JON: When did your cousin arrive from Detroit?

(ask) _____

6. NITA: He just came yesterday.

(tell) _____

7. JON: It's been an incredible winter.

(say) _____

(continued on next page)

8. NITA: The roads may close again with this storm.

(say) _____

9. JON: Don't drive tonight.

(say) _____

10. JON: Stay here with your cousin.

(say) _____

11. NITA: We should try to make it home.

(tell) _____

12. NITA: I have to walk my dog early tomorrow morning.

(say) _____

V. *Read this draft of a news story. There are nine mistakes in the use of direct and indirect speech and embedded questions. Find and correct them. Remember to look at punctuation. The first mistake in already corrected.*

Motorists returning home during last night's snow storm were pleasantly surprised.
Early yesterday afternoon, forecasters had predicted that Route 10 ~~will~~ *would* close because of high winds. However, all major highways remained open last night. One woman, stopping for a newspaper on Woodmere Avenue at about midnight, told this reporter that she and her cousin have almost decided to stay with a friend tonight, rather than drive home. Her cousin told me that I had just arrived from Detroit, where the storm hit first. He said "that it had been a big one." School children seemed especially pleased. Yesterday morning, most schools announced that they will close at 1:00 P.M. Several kids at James Fox Elementary reported that they are planning to spend that afternoon sledding and having snowball fights.

Many people are wondering how could weather forecasters have made such a big mistake. Carla Donati, the weather reporter for WCSX, said that they were not sure why this had happened? The National Weather Service has not commented.

▶ *To check your answers, go to the Answer Key on page 432.*

From Grammar to Writing Using Direct and Indirect Speech

In writing a letter of complaint, we often use both direct and indirect speech to describe a problem. We mostly use indirect speech except when it is important (for 100 percent accuracy) to report someone's exact words or to communicate a speaker's attitude.

 Read this letter of complaint. Underline once all the examples of indirect speech. Underline twice all the examples of direct speech.

Customer Service
One Swell Way
Dallas, TX

Dear Customer Service Representative:

In September 1998, I purchased a computer from your company. After the one-year warranty expired, I bought an extended service contract every year. I always received a renewal notice in the mail that told me <u>that my policy was going to expire in a few weeks</u>. This year, however, I did not receive the notice, and, as a result, I missed the deadline.

Upon realizing this mistake, I immediately called your company and asked if I could renew the service contract. The representative said, <u>"It's too late, Miss."</u> He said that if I wanted to extend my contract, they would have to send someone to my home to inspect my computer. He also told me I would have to pay $160 for this visit. He said that my only other option was to ship my computer back to the company for inspection. I told him that neither of these options was acceptable to me.

When I asked him why I hadn't been notified that my contract was going to expire, he said, "We don't send notices out anymore." I said that I wanted to make a complaint. He said,

(continued on next page)

"Don't complain to me. I don't even park the cars of the people who make these decisions."

I think that your representatives should be more polite when speaking to customers. I also think that your customers should have been told that they would no longer receive renewal notices in the mail. That way, I would not have missed the deadline. I would, therefore, greatly appreciate it if I could have my service contract renewed without having to go through the inconvenience and expense of having my computer inspected. Thank you for your attention.

Sincerely yours,

Anne Marie Clarke

Anne Marie Clarke
Customer No. 5378593

 Look at the letter in Exercise 1. Circle the correct words to complete these sentences. Give an example of each item.

a. The word *that* often introduces <u>direct</u> / (indirect) speech.

    <u>He told me that I would have to pay $160 for this visit.</u>

b. Use quotation marks for <u>direct</u> / <u>indirect</u> speech.

    _____

c. Put final punctuation <u>inside</u> / <u>outside</u> the quotation marks.

    _____

d. You shouldn't use a comma before <u>direct</u> / <u>indirect</u> speech.

    _____

e. Capitalize the first word of <u>direct</u> / <u>indirect</u> speech.

    _____

f. You can leave out the <u>word *that* / question word</u> when it introduces a reported

<u>statement / question</u>.

_____

g. The writer used <u>direct / indirect</u> speech to show that the representative on the

phone was rude.

_____

3 Before you write. Think of an incident you would like to complain about, or make one up. Tell a classmate the story. Answer your classmate's questions. Discuss where to use direct speech most effectively.

4 Write your letter of complaint. Use indirect speech, and, if appropriate, direct speech. Be sure to capitalize and punctuate correctly.

5 Exchange letters with a new partner. Complete the chart for your partner's letter.

a. Do you understand the writer's complaint?	Yes / No
b. Did the writer choose direct speech to show the other person's attitude?	Yes / No
c. Did the writer choose direct speech for 100 percent accuracy?	Yes / No
d. Did the writer use quotation marks for direct speech only?	Yes / No
e. Is the direct speech punctuated correctly?	Yes / No

6 Discuss any problems with your partner. Then rewrite your letter with the necessary corrections.

I. (Units 25–28)
1. **b.** last
2. **a.** would be   **b.** our
3. **a.** told   **b.** they
4. **a.** asked   **b.** was
5. **a.** she   **b.** should bring
6. **a.** told   **b.** not to bring
7. **a.** 'd been   **b.** us
   planning
8. **a.** didn't know   **b.** our
   how
9. **a.** asked   **b.** if there was
10. **a.** not to be
11. **a.** told   **b.** to take
12. **a.** couldn't   **b.** the following
   night
13. **a.** was   **b.** that day
14. **a.** told   **b.** her
15. **a.** had issued   **b.** that night
16. **a.** would   **b.** that day
17. **a.** had to drive
18. **a.** says   **b.** loves
19. **a.** him   **b.** to shovel
20. **a.** asked   **b.** his boots were

II. (Units 25–29)
2. B   5. B   8. C
3. D   6. A   9. D
4. D   7. D   10. C

III. (Units 25–28)
2. D   5. C   8. C
3. A   6. B   9. D
4. B   7. A   10. B

IV. (Units 25–28)
2. Jon told her (that) they had moved in three weeks before.
3. Nita asked if (OR whether) they liked (OR like) that place better than their old apartment.
4. Jon said (that) they liked (OR like) it a lot more.
5. Jon asked (her) when her cousin had arrived from Detroit.
6. Nita told him (that) he had just come the day before.
7. Jon said (that) it had been (OR has been) an incredible winter.

8. Nita said (that) the roads might close again with that storm.
9. Jon said not to drive that night.
10. Jon said to stay there with her cousin.
11. Nita told him (that) they should try to make it home.
12. Nita said (that) she had to walk her dog early the next morning.

V. (Units 25–29)

Motorists returning home during last night's snow storm were pleasantly surprised. Early yesterday afternoon, forecasters had predicted that Route 10 ~~will~~ *would* close because of high winds. However, all major highways remained open last night. One woman, stopping for a newspaper on Woodmere Avenue at about midnight, told this reporter that she and her cousin ~~have~~ *had* almost decided to stay with a friend ~~tonight~~ *that night OR last night*, rather than drive home. Her cousin told me that ~~I~~ *he* had just arrived from Detroit, where the storm hit first. He said ~~"that it had been a big one."~~ *that it had been a big one.* School children seemed especially pleased. Yesterday morning, most schools announced that they ~~will~~ *would* close at 1:00 P.M. Several kids at James Fox Elementary reported that they ~~are~~ *were* planning to spend that afternoon sledding and having snowball fights.

Many people are wondering how ~~could~~ weather forecasters *could* have made such a big mistake. Carla Donati, the weather reporter for WCSX, said that they were not sure why this had happened~~?~~. The National Weather Service has not commented.

APPENDICES

BASE FORM	SIMPLE PAST	PAST PARTICIPLE
arise	arose	arisen
awake	awoke	awoken
be	was/were	been
beat	beat	beaten
become	became	become
begin	began	begun
bend	bent	bent
bet	bet	bet
bite	bit	bitten
bleed	bled	bled
blow	blew	blown
break	broke	broken
bring	brought	brought
build	built	built
burn	burned/burnt	burned/burnt
burst	burst	burst
buy	bought	bought
catch	caught	caught
choose	chose	chosen
cling	clung	clung
come	came	come
cost	cost	cost
creep	crept	crept
cut	cut	cut
deal	dealt	dealt
dig	dug	dug
dive	dived/dove	dived
do	did	done
draw	drew	drawn
dream	dreamed/dreamt	dreamed/dreamt
drink	drank	drunk
drive	drove	driven
eat	ate	eaten
fall	fell	fallen
feed	fed	fed
feel	felt	felt
fight	fought	fought
find	found	found
fit	fit	fit
flee	fled	fled
fling	flung	flung
fly	flew	flown
forbid	forbade/forbad	forbidden
forget	forgot	forgotten
forgive	forgave	forgiven
freeze	froze	frozen
get	got	gotten/got
give	gave	given
go	went	gone

BASE FORM	SIMPLE PAST	PAST PARTICIPLE
grind	ground	ground
grow	grew	grown
hang	hung	hung
have	had	had
hear	heard	heard
hide	hid	hidden
hit	hit	hit
hold	held	held
hurt	hurt	hurt
keep	kept	kept
kneel	knelt	knelt
knit	knit/knitted	knit/knitted
know	knew	known
lay	laid	laid
lead	led	led
leap	leapt	leapt
leave	left	left
lend	lent	lent
let	let	let
lie (lie down)	lay	lain
light	lit/lighted	lit/lighted
lose	lost	lost
make	made	made
mean	meant	meant
meet	met	met
pay	paid	paid
prove	proved	proved/proven
put	put	put
quit	quit	quit
read /rid/	read /rɛd/	read /rɛd/
ride	rode	ridden
ring	rang	rung
rise	rose	risen
run	ran	run
say	said	said
see	saw	seen
seek	sought	sought
sell	sold	sold
send	sent	sent
set	set	set
sew	sewed	sewn/sewed
shake	shook	shaken
shave	shaved	shaved/shaven
shine	shone	shone
shoot	shot	shot
show	showed	shown
shrink	shrank/shrunk	shrunk/shrunken
shut	shut	shut
sing	sang	sung

(continued on next page)

BASE FORM	SIMPLE PAST	PAST PARTICIPLE		BASE FORM	SIMPLE PAST	PAST PARTICIPLE
sink	sank	sunk		sweep	swept	swept
sit	sat	sat		swim	swam	swum
sleep	slept	slept		swing	swung	swung
slide	slid	slid		take	took	taken
speak	spoke	spoken		teach	taught	taught
speed	sped	sped		tear	tore	torn
spend	spent	spent		tell	told	told
spill	spilled/spilt	spilled/spilt		think	thought	thought
spin	spun	spun		throw	threw	thrown
spit	spit/spat	spat		understand	understood	understood
split	split	split		upset	upset	upset
spread	spread	spread		wake	woke	woken
spring	sprang	sprung		wear	wore	worn
stand	stood	stood		weave	wove	woven
steal	stole	stolen		weep	wept	wept
stick	stuck	stuck		win	won	won
sting	stung	stung		wind	wound	wound
stink	stank/stunk	stunk		withdraw	withdrew	withdrawn
strike	struck	struck		wring	wrung	wrung
swear	swore	sworn		write	wrote	written

② Common Non-action (Stative) Verbs

EMOTIONS	MENTAL STATES		WANTS AND PREFERENCES	APPEARANCE AND VALUE	POSSESSION AND RELATIONSHIP
admire	agree	know	desire	appear	belong
adore	assume	mean	need	be	contain
appreciate	believe	mind	prefer	cost	have
care	consider	presume	want	equal	own
detest	disagree	realize	wish	feel	possess
dislike	disbelieve	recognize		look	
doubt	estimate	remember	**PERCEPTION AND THE SENSES**	matter	
envy	expect	see (*understand*)	feel	represent	
fear	feel (*believe*)	suppose	hear	resemble	
hate	find	suspect	notice	seem	
hope	guess	think (*believe*)	observe	signify	
like	hesitate	understand	perceive	smell	
love	hope	wonder	see	sound	
regret	imagine		smell	taste	
respect			taste	weigh	
trust					

③ Common Verbs Followed by the Gerund (Base Form of Verb + -*ing*)

acknowledge	consider	endure	give up (*stop*)	miss	quit	resist
admit	delay	enjoy	imagine	postpone	recall	risk
advise	deny	escape	justify	practice	recommend	suggest
appreciate	detest	explain	keep (*continue*)	prevent	regret	support
avoid	discontinue	feel like	mention	prohibit	report	tolerate
can't help	discuss	finish	mind (*object to*)	propose	resent	understand
celebrate	dislike	forgive				

4 Common Verbs Followed by the Infinitive (*To* + Base Form of Verb)

afford	can('t) afford	expect	hurry	neglect	promise	volunteer
agree	can('t) wait	fail	intend	offer	refuse	wait
appear	choose	grow	learn	pay	request	want
arrange	consent	help	manage	plan	seem	wish
ask	decide	hesitate	mean	prepare	struggle	would like
attempt	deserve	hope	need	pretend	swear	yearn

5 Verbs Followed by Objects and the Infinitive

advise	challenge	encourage	get	need*	persuade	require	want*
allow	choose*	expect*	help*	order	promise*	teach	warn
ask*	convince	forbid	hire	pay*	remind	tell	wish*
cause	enable	force	invite	permit	request	urge	would like*

*These verbs can also be followed by the infinitive without an object (example: *ask to leave* or *ask someone to leave*).

6 Common Verbs Followed by the Gerund or the Infinitive

begin	continue	hate	love	remember*	stop*
can't stand	forget*	like	prefer	start	try

*These verbs can be followed by either the gerund or the infinitive but there is a big difference in meaning.

7 Common Verb + Preposition Combinations

admit to	believe in	count on	insist on	rely on	talk about
advise against	choose between/	deal with	look forward to	resort to	think about
apologize for	among	dream about/of	object to	succeed in	wonder about
approve of	complain about	feel like/about	plan on		

8 Common Adjective + Preposition Expressions

be accustomed to	be capable of	be fed up with	be pleased about	be slow at
be afraid of	be careful of	be fond of	be ready for	be sorry for/about
be amazed at/by	be concerned about	be glad about	be responsible for	be surprised at/
be angry at	be content with	be good at	be sad about	about/by
be ashamed of	be curious about	be happy about	be safe from	be terrible at
be aware of	be different from	be interested in	be satisfied with	be tired of
be awful at	be excited about	be nervous about	be shocked at/by	be used to
be bad at	be famous for	be opposed to	be sick of	be worried about
be bored with/by				

9 Common Adjectives that Can Be Followed by the Infinitive*

afraid	anxious	depressed	disturbed	encouraged	happy	pleased	reluctant	surprised
alarmed	ashamed	determined	eager	excited	hesitant	proud	sad	touched
amazed	curious	disappointed	easy	fortunate	likely	ready	shocked	upset
angry	delighted	distressed	embarrassed	glad	lucky	relieved	sorry	willing

*Example: *I'm happy to hear that.*

⑩ Irregular Comparisons of Adjectives, Adverbs, and Quantifiers

ADJECTIVE	ADVERB	COMPARATIVE	SUPERLATIVE
bad	badly	worse	worst
far	far	farther/further	farthest/furthest
good	well	better	best
little	little	less	least
many/a lot of	—	more	most
much*/a lot of	much*/a lot	more	most

Much is usually only used in questions and negative statements.

⑪ Common Participial Adjectives

-ed	-ing	-ed	-ing	-ed	-ing
alarmed	alarming	disturbed	disturbing	moved	moving
amazed	amazing	embarrassed	embarrassing	paralyzed	paralyzing
amused	amusing	entertained	entertaining	pleased	pleasing
annoyed	annoying	excited	exciting	relaxed	relaxing
astonished	astonishing	exhausted	exhausting	satisfied	satisfying
bored	boring	fascinated	fascinating	shocked	shocking
confused	confusing	frightened	frightening	surprised	surprising
depressed	depressing	horrified	horrifying	terrified	terrifying
disappointed	disappointing	inspired	inspiring	tired	tiring
disgusted	disgusting	interested	interesting	touched	touching
distressed	distressing	irritated	irritating	troubled	troubling

⑫ Some Adjectives that Form the Comparative and Superlative in Two Ways

ADJECTIVE	COMPARATIVE	SUPERLATIVE
common	commoner / more common	commonest / most common
cruel	crueler / more cruel	cruelest / most cruel
deadly	deadlier / more deadly	deadliest / most deadly
friendly	friendlier / more friendly	friendliest / most friendly
handsome	handsomer / more handsome	handsomest / most handsome
happy	happier / more happy	happiest / most happy
likely	likelier / more likely	likeliest / most likely
lively	livelier / more lively	liveliest / most lively
lonely	lonelier / more lonely	loneliest / most lonely
lovely	lovelier / more lovely	loveliest / most lovely
narrow	narrower / more narrow	narrowest / most narrow
pleasant	pleasanter / more pleasant	pleasantest / most pleasant
polite	politer / more polite	politest / most polite
quiet	quieter / more quiet	quietest / most quiet
shallow	shallower / more shallow	shallowest / most shallow
sincere	sincerer / more sincere	sincerest / most sincere
stupid	stupider / more stupid	stupidest / most stupid
true	truer / more true	truest / most true

13 Common Reporting Verbs

STATEMENTS

acknowledge	claim	indicate	reply
add	complain	maintain	report
admit	conclude	mean	say
announce	confess	note	state
answer	declare	observe	suggest
argue	deny	promise	tell
assert	exclaim	remark	warn
believe	explain	repeat	write

INSTRUCTIONS, COMMANDS REQUESTS, AND INVITATIONS

advise	invite
ask	order
caution	say
command	tell
demand	urge
instruct	warn

QUESTIONS

ask
inquire
question
want to know
wonder

14 Verbs and Expressions Commonly Used Reflexively

amuse oneself	be proud of oneself	dry oneself	introduce oneself	remind oneself
ask oneself	behave oneself	enjoy oneself	kill oneself	see oneself
avail oneself of	believe in oneself	feel sorry for oneself	look after oneself	take care of oneself
be hard on oneself	blame oneself	help oneself	look at oneself	talk to oneself
be oneself	cut oneself	hurt oneself	pride oneself on	teach oneself
be pleased with oneself	deprive oneself of	imagine oneself	push oneself	tell oneself

15 Some Common Transitive Phrasal Verbs

(s.o. = someone s.t. = something)

Note: *Separable phrasal verbs are shown with the object between the verb and the particle (call s.o. up). Inseparable phrasal verbs are shown with the object after the particle (carry on s.t.). Verbs which must be separated are shown with an asterisk (*) (do s.t. over). Other separable verbs can take the noun object either between the verb and the particle or after the particle (call Jan up OR call up Jan). These verbs must, however, be separated by a pronoun object (call her up NOT ~~call up her~~).*

PHRASAL VERB	MEANING	PHRASAL VERB	MEANING
ask s.o. **over***	invite to one's home	**close** s.t. **down**	close by force
block s.t. **out**	stop from passing through (light/ noise)	**come off** s.t.	become unattached
		come up with s.t.	invent
blow s.t. **out**	stop burning by blowing on it	**count on** s.o. or s.t.	depend on
blow s.t. **up**	1. make explode	**cover** s.o. or s.t. **up**	cover completely
	2. fill with air (a balloon/water toy)	**cross** s.t. **out**	draw a line through
	3. make something larger (a photograph)	**cut** s.t. **down**	bring down by cutting (a tree)
		cut s.t. **off**	1. stop the supply of
bring s.t. **about**	make happen		2. remove by cutting
bring s.o. or s.t. **back**	return		
bring s.o. **down***	depress	**cut** s.t. **out**	remove by cutting
bring s.t. **out**	introduce (a new product/book)	**do** s.t. **over***	do again
bring s.o. **up**	raise (children)	**do** s.o. or s.t. **up**	make more beautiful
bring s.t. **up**	bring attention to	**draw** s.t. **together**	unite
burn s.t. **down**	burn completely	**dream** s.t. **up**	invent
call s.o. **back**	return a phone call	**drink** s.t. **up**	drink completely
call s.o. **in**	ask for help with a problem	**drop** s.o. or s.t. **off**	take someplace
call s.t. **off**	cancel	**drop out of** s.t.	quit
call s.o. **up**	phone	**empty** s.t. **out**	empty completely
carry on s.t.	continue	**figure** s.o. or s.t. **out**	understand (after thinking about)
carry s.t. **out**	conduct (an experiment/a plan)	**fill** s.t. **in**	complete with information
charge s.t. **up**	charge with electricity	**fill** s.t. **out**	complete (a form)
cheer s.o. **up**	cause to feel happier	**fill** s.t. **up**	fill completely
clean s.o. or s.t. **up**	clean completely	**find** s.t. **out**	learn information
clear s.t. **up**	clarify	**follow through with** s.t.	complete
		get s.t. **across**	get people to understand an idea

(continued on next page)

PHRASAL VERB	MEANING	PHRASAL VERB	MEANING
get out of s.t.	leave (a car/taxi)	see s.t. **through***	complete
get s.t. **out of** s.t.*	benefit from	set s.t. **off**	cause to explode
give s.t. **away**	give without charging money	set s.t. **up**	1. prepare for use
give s.t. **back**	return		2. establish (a business/an organization)
give s.t. **out**	distribute	show s.o. or s.t. **off**	display the best qualities
give s.t. **up**	quit, abandon	shut s.t. **off**	stop (a machine/light)
go **after** s.o. or s.t.	pursue	start s.t. **over***	start again
go **along with** s.t.	support	stick **with/to** s.o. or s.t.	not quit, not leave
hand s.t. **in**	submit work (to a boss/teacher)	straighten s.t. **up**	make neat
hand s.t. **out**	distribute	switch s.t. **on**	start (a machine/light)
hang s.t. **up**	put on a hook or hanger	take s.t. **away**	remove
help s.o. **out**	assist	take s.o. or s.t. **back**	return
hold s.t. **on**	keep attached	take s.t. **down**	remove
keep s.o. or s.t. **away**	cause to stay at a distance	take s.t. **in**	notice, understand, and remember
keep s.t. **on***	not remove (a piece of clothing/jewelry)	take s.t. **off**	remove
keep **up with** s.o. or s.t.	go as fast as	take s.o. **on**	hire
lay s.o. **off**	end employment	take s.t. **on**	agree to do
lay s.t. **out**	1. spend (money)	take s.t. **out**	borrow from a library
	2. arrange according to a plan	talk s.o. **into***	persuade
leave s.t. **on**	1. not turn off (a light/radio)	talk s.t. **over**	discuss
	2. not remove (a piece of clothing/jewelry)	team **up with** s.o.	start to work with
leave s.t. **out**	omit	tear s.t. **down**	destroy
let s.o. **down**	disappoint	tear s.t. **up**	tear into small pieces
let s.o. or s.t. **in**	allow to enter	think **back on** s.o. or s.t.	remember
let s.o. **off**	allow to leave (a bus/car)	think s.t. **over**	consider
let s.o. or s.t. **out**	allow to leave	think s.t. **up**	invent
light s.t. **up**	illuminate	throw s.t. **away/out**	discard
look s.o. or s.t. **over**	examine	touch s.t. **up**	improve by making small changes
look s.t. **up**	try to find (in a book/on the Internet)	try s.t. **on**	put clothing on to see if it fits
make s.t. **up**	create	try s.t. **out**	use to see if it works
move s.t. **around**	change the location	turn s.t. **around**	change the direction so the front is at the back
pass s.t. **out**	distribute	turn s.o. or s.t. **down**	reject
pass s.o. or s.t. **up**	decide not to use	turn s.t. **down**	lower the volume (a TV/radio)
pay s.o. or s.t. **back**	repay	turn s.t. **in**	submit
pick s.o. or s.t. **out**	1. select	turn s.o. or s.t. **into***	change from one form to another
	2. identify	turn s.o. **off**	(slang) destroy interest
pick s.o. or s.t. **up**	lift	turn s.t. **off**	stop (a machine/light)
pick s.t. **up**	get (an idea/a new book/an interest)	turn s.t. **on**	start (a machine/light)
point s.o. or s.t. **out**	indicate	turn s.t. **over**	turn something so the top side is at the bottom
put s.t. **away**	put in an appropriate place	turn s.t. **up**	raise the volume (a TV/radio)
put s.t. **back**	return to its original place	use s.t. **up**	use completely, consume
put s.o. or s.t. **down**	stop holding	wake s.o. **up**	awaken
put s.t. **off**	postpone	work s.t. **off**	remove by work or activity
put s.t. **on**	cover the body	work s.t. **out**	solve
put s.t. **together**	assemble	write s.t. **down**	write on a piece of paper
put s.t. **up**	erect	write s.t. **up**	write in a finished form
run **into** s.o.	meet accidentally		

16 Some Common Intransitive Phrasal Verbs

PHRASAL VERB	MEANING	PHRASAL VERB	MEANING
blow up	explode	burn down	burn completely
break down	stop functioning	call back	return a phone call
break out	occur suddenly	catch on	become popular

(continued on next page)

PHRASAL VERB	MEANING	PHRASAL VERB	MEANING
clear up	become clear	go over	succeed with an audience
close down	stop operating	go up	be built
come about	happen	grow up	become an adult
come along	accompany	hang up	end a phone call
come back	return	hold on	1. wait
come in	enter		2. not hang up the phone
come off	become unattached	keep away	stay at a distance
come out	appear	keep on	continue
come up	arise	keep up	go as fast as
dress up	wear special clothes	lie down	recline
drop in	visit unexpectedly	light up	illuminate
drop out	quit	look out	be careful
eat out	eat in a restaurant	make up	reconcile
empty out	empty completely	pay off	be worthwhile
end up	1. do something unexpected or unintended	pick up	improve
	2. reach a final place or condition	play around	have fun
		run out	not have enough of
fall off	become detached	show up	appear
find out	learn information	sign up	register
follow through	complete	sit down	take a seat
fool around	act playful	slip up	make a mistake
get ahead	make progress, succeed	stand up	rise
get along	relate well	start over	start again
get back	return	stay up	remain awake
get by	survive	straighten up	make neat
get together	meet	take off	depart (a plane)
get up	rise from bed	turn out	have a particular result
give up	quit	turn up	appear
go back	return	wake up	arise after sleeping
go off	explode (a gun/fireworks/a rocket)	watch out	be careful
go on	continue	work out	1. be resolved
go out	leave		2. exercise

⓱ Spelling Rules for the Present Progressive

1. Add -ing to the base form of the verb.

   read   reading
   stand   standing

2. If a verb ends in a silent -e, drop the final -e and add -ing.

   leave   leaving
   take   taking

3. In a one-syllable word, if the last three letters are a consonant-vowel-consonant combination (CVC), double the last consonant before adding -ing.

   C V C
   ↓ ↓ ↓
   s i t   sitting
   C V C
   ↓ ↓ ↓
   r u n   running

   However, do not double the last consonant in words that end in w, x, or y.

   sew   sewing
   fix   fixing
   enjoy   enjoying

4. In words of two or more syllables that end in a consonant-vowel-consonant combination, double the last consonant only if the last syllable is stressed.

   admít   admitting   (The last syllable is stressed)
   whisper   whispering   (The last syllable is not stressed, so you don't double the -r.)

5. If a verb ends in -ie, change the ie to y before adding -ing.

   die   dying

18 Spelling Rules for the Simple Present Tense: Third-Person Singular *(he, she, it)*

1. Add *-s* for most verbs.

   work   work*s*
   buy   buy*s*
   ride   ride*s*
   return   return*s*

2. Add *-es* for words that end in *-ch, -s, -sh, -x,* or *-z.*

   watch   watch*es*
   pass   pass*es*
   rush   rush*es*
   relax   relax*es*
   buzz   buzz*es*

3. Change the *y* to *i* and add *-es* when the base form ends in a consonant + *y*.

   study   stud*ies*
   hurry   hurr*ies*
   dry   dr*ies*

   Do not change the *y* when the base form ends in a vowel + *y*. Add *-s.*

   play   play*s*
   enjoy   enjoy*s*

4. A few verbs have irregular forms.

   be   is
   do   does
   go   goes
   have   has

19 Spelling Rules for the Simple Past Tense of Regular Verbs

1. If the verb ends in a consonant, add *-ed.*

   return   return*ed*
   help   help*ed*

2. If the verb ends in *-e*, add *-d.*

   live   live*d*
   create   create*d*
   die   die*d*

3. In one-syllable words, if the verb ends in a consonant-vowel-consonant combination (CVC), double the final consonant and add *-ed.*

   C V C
   ↓ ↓ ↓
   h o p   hop*ped*
   C V C
   ↓ ↓ ↓
   r u b   rub*bed*

   However, do not double one-syllable words ending in *-w, -x,* or *-y.*

   bow   bow*ed*
   mix   mix*ed*
   play   play*ed*

4. In words of two or more syllables that end in a consonant-vowel-consonant combination, double the last consonant only if the last syllable is stressed.

   prefér   prefer*red*   (The last syllable is stressed.)
   vísit   visit*ed*   (The last syllable is not stressed, so you don't double the *t.*)

5. If the verb ends in a consonant + *y*, change the *y* to *i* and add *-ed.*

   worry   worr*ied*
   carry   carr*ied*

6. If the verb ends in a vowel + *y*, add *-ed.* (Do not change the *y* to *i*.)

   play   play*ed*
   annoy   annoy*ed*

   Exceptions: pay—paid,   lay—laid,   say—said

20 Spelling Rules for the Comparative *(-er)* and Superlative *(-est)* of Adjectives

1. Add *-er* to one-syllable adjectives to form the comparative. Add *-est* to one-syllable adjectives to form the superlative.

   cheap   cheap*er*   cheap*est*
   bright   bright*er*   bright*est*

2. If the adjective ends in *-e*, add *-r* or *-st.*

   nice   nic*er*   nic*est*

3. If the adjective ends in a consonant + *y*, change *y* to *i* before you add *-er* or *-est.*

                 pretty   prett*ier*   prett*iest*
   Exception: shy   shy*er*   shy*est*

4. If the adjective ends in a consonant-vowel-consonant combination (CVC), double the final consonant before adding *-er* or *-est.*

   C V C
   ↓ ↓ ↓
   b i g   big*ger*   big*gest*

   However, do not double the consonant in words ending in *-w* or *-y.*

   slow   slow*er*   slow*est*
   coy   coy*er*   coy*est*

21 Spelling Rules for Adverbs Ending in *-ly*

1. Add *-ly* to the corresponding adjective.

nice	nice*ly*
quiet	quiet*ly*
beautiful	beautiful*ly*

2. If the adjective ends in a consonant + *y*, change the *y* to *i* before adding *-ly*.

easy	eas*ily*

3. If the adjective ends in *-le*, drop the *e* and add *-y*.

possible	possibl*y*

However, do not drop the *e* for other adjectives ending in *-e*.

	extreme	extreme*ly*
Exception:	true	tru*ly*

4. If the adjective ends in *-ic*, add *-ally*.

basic	basic*ally*
fantastic	fantastic*ally*

22 Punctuation Rules for Direct Speech

Direct speech may either follow or come before the reporting verb. When direct speech follows the reporting verb,

a. Put a comma after the reporting verb.
b. Use opening quotation marks (") before the first word of the direct speech.
c. Begin the quotation with a capital letter.
d. Use the appropriate end punctuation for the direct speech. It may be a period (.), a question mark (?), or an exclamation point (!).
e. Put closing quotation marks (") after the end punctuation of the quotation.

Examples: He said, "I had a good time."
She asked, "Where's the party?"
They shouted, "Be careful!"

When direct speech comes before the reporting verb,

a. Begin the sentence with opening quotation marks (").
b. Use the appropriate end punctuation for the direct speech. If the direct speech is a statement, use a comma (,). If the direct speech is a question, use a question mark (?). If the direct speech is an exclamation, use an exclamation point (!).
c. Use closing quotation marks after the end punctuation for the direct speech (").
d. Begin the reporting clause with a lower-case letter.
e. Use a period at the end of the main sentence (.).

Examples: "I had a good time," he said.
"Where's the party?" she asked.
"Be careful!" they shouted.

23 Pronunciation Table

These are the pronunciation symbols used in this text. Listen to the pronunciation of the key words.

VOWELS				CONSONANTS			
Symbol	Key Word	Symbol	Key Word	Symbol	Key Word	Symbol	Key Word
i	beat, feed	ə	banana, among	p	pack, happy	ʃ	ship, machine, station, special, discussion
ɪ	bit, did	ɚ	shirt, murder	b	back, rubber		
eɪ	date, paid	aɪ	bite, cry, buy, eye	t	tie	ʒ	measure, vision
ɛ	bet, bed			d	die	h	hot, who
æ	bat, bad	aʊ	about, how	k	came, key, quick	m	men
ɑ	box, odd, father	ɔɪ	voice, boy	g	game, guest	n	sun, know, pneumonia
ɔ	bought, dog	ɪr	beer	tʃ	church, nature, watch	ŋ	sung, ringing
oʊ	boat, road	ɛr	bare	dʒ	judge, general, major	w	wet, white
ʊ	book, good	ɑr	bar	f	fan, photograph	l	light, long
u	boot, food, student	ɔr	door	v	van	r	right, wrong
ʌ	but, mud, mother	ʊr	tour	θ	thing, breath	y	yes, use, music
				ð	then, breathe	ţ	butter, bottle
				s	sip, city, psychology		
				z	zip, please, goes		

STRESS
' shows main stress.

24 Pronunciation Rules for the Simple Present Tense: Third-Person Singular (he, she, it)

1. The third person singular in the simple present tense always ends in the letter -s. There are, however, three different pronunciations for the final sound of the third person singular.

/s/	/z/	/ɪz/
talks	loves	dances

2. The final sound is pronounced /s/ after the voiceless sounds /p/, /t/, /k/, and /f/.

top	tops
get	gets
take	takes
laugh	laughs

3. The final sound is pronounced /z/ after the voiced sounds /b/, /d/, /g/, /v/, /ð/, /m/, /n/, /ŋ/, /l/, and /r/.

describe	describes
spend	spends
hug	hugs
live	lives
bathe	bathes
seem	seems
remain	remains
sing	sings
tell	tells
lower	lowers

4. The final sound is pronounced /z/ after all vowel sounds.

agree	agrees
try	tries
stay	stays
know	knows

5. The final sound is pronounced /ɪz/ after the sounds /s/, /z/, /ʃ/, /ʒ/, /tʃ/, and /dʒ/. /ɪz/ adds a syllable to the verb.

relax	relaxes
freeze	freezes
rush	rushes
massage	massages
watch	watches
judge	judges

6. *Do* and *say* have a change in vowel sound.

say	/sɛɪ/	says	/sɛz/
do	/du/	does	/dʌz/

25 Pronunciation Rules for the Simple Past Tense of Regular Verbs

1. The regular simple past always ends in the letter -d. There are, however, three different pronunciations for the final sound of the regular simple past.

/t/	/d/	/ɪd/
raced	lived	attended

2. The final sound is pronounced /t/ after the voiceless sounds /p/, /k/, /f/, /s/, /ʃ/, and /tʃ/.

hop	hopped
work	worked
laugh	laughed
address	addressed
publish	published
watch	watched

3. The final sound is pronounced /d/ after the voiced sounds /b/, /g/, /v/, /z/, /ʒ/, /dʒ/, /m/, /n/, /ŋ /, /l/, /r/, and /ð/.

rub	rubbed
hug	hugged
live	lived
surprise	surprised
massage	massaged
change	changed
rhyme	rhymed
return	returned
bang	banged
enroll	enrolled
appear	appeared
bathe	bathed

4. The final sound is pronounced /d/ after all vowel sounds.

agree	agreed
play	played
die	died
enjoy	enjoyed

5. The final sound is pronounced /ɪd/ after /t/ and /d/. /ɪd/ adds a syllable to the verb.

start	started
decide	decided

INDEX

This Index is for the full and split editions. All entries are in the full book.
Entries for Volume A of the split edition are in black. Entries for Volume B are in color.